MARY BOYKIN
CHESNUT

AMERICAN PROFILES

Norman K. Risjord,
Series Editor

MARY BOYKIN CHESNUT

A Confederate Woman's Life

Mary A. DeCredico

MADISON HOUSE

Madison 1996

DeCredico, Mary A.
Mary Boykin Chesnut
A Confederate Woman's Life

LIBRARY OF CONGRESS CATALOGING-IN-PUBLICATION DATA

DeCredico, Mary A.
Mary Boykin Chesnut : a Confederate woman's life / Mary A.
DeCredico. — 1st ed.
p.   cm. — (American profiles)
Includes bibliographical references and index.
ISBN 0-945612-46-x (cloth : acid-free paper). —
ISBN 0-945612-47-8 (pbk. : acid-free paper)
1. Chesnut, Mary Boykin Miller, 1823–1886.   2. South Carolina—
Biography.   3. Confederate States of America—Biography.
I. Title.   II. Series: American profiles (Madison, Wis.)
F273.C54D43   1995
975.7'041'092—dc20
[B]   95-11155
                                                                                    CIP

Typeset in Fairfield, Berthold Walbaum, and ITC Fenice
Designed by William Kasdorf

Printed in the United States of America
on acid-free paper by Edwards Brothers, Inc.

Published by Madison House Publishers, Inc.
P.O. Box 3100, Madison, Wisconsin, 53704

FIRST EDITION

To two strong northern ladies,
my grandmothers,
Ruth Jack and Mary DeCredico,
who taught me grace and perseverance

Contents

Illustrations

Editor's Foreword

THE COMPLAINT OF MANY PEOPLE who dislike history is that it is full of obscure names, arcane dates, and big words that always seem to end in "ism." The problem is that history, in some ways, is like a foreign language. The grammar has to be mastered before thought, discussion, and interpretation is possible. The task confronting the teacher of history is how to sugarcoat the pill.

For some years I have given a talk to educators at meetings and seminars around the country entitled "Making History Human." It is essentially a pitch for a biographical approach as a pedagogical device. I am not advocating the reduction of history to a series of human-interest stories. My thesis, instead, is that complex and often dry subjects (when presented in general terms) can be enlivened and given meaning through a focus on one of the individual stories. For example, P. T. Barnum's impact on popular amusements can add a new dimension to the concept of democracy in nineteenth-century America. The story of Jackie Robinson (or Satchell Paige?) can add poignancy to the often legalistic (because of its emphasis on statutes and court decisions) story of civil rights in the middle decades of the twentieth century.

That is the basic purpose of Madison House's *American Profiles* series—to add a human dimension to the study of history. *American Profiles* offers relatively concise and swiftly-paced sketches that contribute significantly to the discourse on the American past. Each narrative takes advantage of the explosion of recent historiography while the author's interpretive insights serve as a basis for organizing that mass of complex and often disparate information.

What we hope to do with the books in the *American Profiles* series is to tell the American story—to tell the multitude of our national stories. Our goal is to arouse interest and provoke thought. Once that is accomplished, we can truly begin to teach our history.

NORMAN K. RISJORD
Series Editor

Acknowledgments

THIS BOOK BEGAN AS A SUGGESTION of Professor Norman Risjord, general editor for Madison House's *American Profiles* series. Believing correctly that Mary Boykin Chesnut's diary was a boundless source of information about that remarkable woman and the South, Norm encouraged me to think about Mary Chesnut as a fit subject for the *Profiles* series. I agreed with his proposal, and the concept of Mary Chesnut as a vehicle for understanding the white Southern elite of the Civil War era was born. Throughout the project Norm has been a source of great help and advice, editing clunky prose and suggesting other ways to approach the subject. Gregory M. Britton, the director of Madison House, has also been a great source of cooperation and support from the inception of this project. Indeed, I could not have wished for more support from an editor and a publisher.

Much of the research for this book was accomplished thanks to the United States Naval Academy, which granted me a sabbatical from teaching and administrative duties one semester. During the course of researching and writing, a number of people provided valuable insight and suggestions. Parts of the book were submitted to the Naval Academy Department of History's works-in-progress seminar, where it was subjected to a close and critical analysis by many of my colleagues. As usual, they forced me to reassess and recast several of my arguments. Richard Abels deserves special mention as one who has helped me sort out Mary Chesnut and some of the larger issues posed by this study. His careful reading and perceptive comments and criticisms have been exceedingly helpful throughout this entire process.

The manuscript also benefited from George C. Rable's comments and critiques. He, too, forced me to clarify, rethink, and flesh out key concepts of the Confederate era, which made the final version clearer and more detailed. Any errors that remain are mine alone.

The debts a researcher and writer owe archival and library personnel are enormous, and my debts are no different. The library staffs at the University of South Carolina's South Caroliniana Library and the South Carolina Historical Society were instrumental in helping me locate manuscript materials dealing with the Chesnuts, South Carolina society and politics, and the wartime scene. The inter-library loan office at the Naval Academy continues to be a source of aid and assistance, always locating speedily and effortlessly obscure and dated books, as well as the most recent monographs.

The illustrations which grace this volume were reproduced thanks to the assistance of several organizations and individuals. I am indebted to Mrs. Martha Daniels of Camden, South Carolina, for the lovely photographs of Mulberry plantation; to the U.S. Army Military History Institute at Carlisle Barracks, Pennsylvania; to the Library of Congress; and to the South Caroliniana Library. William J. Clipson of Annapolis, Maryland, helped me trace Mary Chesnut's refugee route, and drew the maps of that journey and of South Carolina in 1860.

As always, family and friends proved essential to the successful completion of this project. My father, in particular, speeded me to finish if only so I would not have to answer his weekly queries as to "how's Chesnut coming along?" The love and support of everyone at home, at the office, and elsewhere, helped me more than they can possibly know. To all of them, I extend my heartfelt thanks.

M. A. D.
United States Naval Academy
November 1995

Introduction

> I do not allow myself vain regrets or sad foreboding. This southern
> confederacy must be supported now by calm determination—&
> cool brains. We have risked all, & we must play our best for the
> stake is life or death.

THUS BEGINS MARY BOYKIN CHESNUT'S CIVIL WAR DIARY, one of the
most remarkable accounts of the South during the Civil War era
ever written. Over the years, Mary's diary, in various forms and
renderings, has enlightened and delighted scholars and students
alike. In the pages of her diary, Mary records the full life and times
of the Southern Confederacy. In Montgomery, Alabama, at its founding, on a hotel roof in Charleston during the bombardment of Fort
Sumter, within the "inner circle" at the White House of the Confederacy in Richmond, as a close friend and confidante of some of the
South's most important and influential people, Mary Chesnut, was,
in virtually every instance, a participant in and observer of the
Southern Confederacy's birth, short life, and demise. Thanks to her
observations, sometimes witty, always interesting and insightful, we
can chronicle the reaction of wealthy white Southerners to the rise
and fall of the Confederate nation.

In many ways, Mary Chesnut is both a typical and atypical
member of the antebellum and wartime southern elite. Born into
the aristocracy of South Carolina, she received all the benefits of
wealth—education at an exclusive boarding school in Charleston,

instruction into the social graces of the planter class, marriage into another prominent South Carolina family, and life on the plantation surrounded by black slaves. Her wartime experiences were decidedly atypical, for she moved within a circle of political and social privilege. Because her husband was an advisor to President Jefferson Davis, Mary had the opportunity to observe every aspect of the Confederate experience from Richmond. Throughout this period, she also had the good fortune to have the financial means to continue leading a life of leisure and elegance that she craved and loved best.

Invasion and defeat brought experiences of hardship and poverty to her life, problems that more than a few southern planters also faced. Forced out of her homes in Columbia and Camden, South Carolina, Mary fled to North Carolina to avoid the menace of General William T. Sherman's army in 1865. With peace, Mary and her husband returned to the Chesnut family plantation to find it partially in ruins. Worse still, the Chesnut money had been invested in Confederate notes and bonds rendered worthless by the defeat. Faced with mounting debts, the loss of their labor force, and a dim future, Mary and James Chesnut struggled to recoup and recover in the turbulent years of Reconstruction. They never really succeeded in re-establishing themselves as wealthy and powerful members of South Carolina society. When Mary died in 1886, she left behind only her home, the small egg and dairy business she used to eke out a living after the war, and her writings.

Mary Chesnut's life and experiences, as recorded in her Civil War journals, and in the novels she penned after the war, provide a striking glimpse into the the life of a privileged and perceptive southern lady. In most respects, she defies the southern belle stereotype, for she was no vapid, dim-witted flirt. Rather, she was a woman of intelligence, strength, charm and grace, who was well-read on myriad topics, and who could be equally at ease at a formal soiree or a political debate. On almost every occasion during the war, she found herself surrounded by important, powerful men, but she was rarely intimidated by them; in fact, she usually impressed them with her interest in and knowledge of things military and governmental.

One cannot help but be struck by the breadth of her knowledge or the extent of her interests. Her diary conveys her ecleticism: it is full of descriptions of various literary works, from Thackeray to Balzac, and her impressions of them; it contains poetry and passages in French, a language Mary spoke fluently; and it carries on a dialogue of praise for Jefferson Davis and curses for his detractors.

Mary Chesnut did have her selfish, self-indulgent side. Her love of parties led to numerous quarrels with her rather stiff and proper husband. During the darkest days of the Confederacy's life she exhibited a blithe disregard for the horrors of war and their effect on society's less fortunate. Still, she did contribute to the southern war effort. As women did throughout the South, she embraced the cause of aiding the sick and wounded, and worked daily in hospitals in both Virginia and South Carolina. It was not an easy experience, but she bore it with a sense of duty and noblesse oblige.

In many ways, Mary Boykin Chesnut's life parallels that of another strong-willed, independent minded Southern woman of wealth and status. Like Margaret Mitchell's fictional Scarlett O'Hara, Mary was "to the manor born." She moved among all the elite circles; she embraced the Confederate cause with fervor; she watched as the dream of independence grew dim and died; she was forced to flee the dreaded Yankees and returned to find her world and her home destroyed; and she refused to surrender her principles or beliefs during the period of Reconstruction. Unlike Scarlett, Mary never lived to see the Chesnut family fortune rebuilt. She died over thirty years after Appomattox and had little to leave that would indicate how prosperous and prominent she had once been. Still, the record of her life could have served as a model for Margaret Mitchell as she created her much-loved heroine. Mary had the charm, intelligence, and independence that Scarlett exhibited again and again.

But Mary Chesnut is a real historical figure, and that makes her story even more compelling than a fictional creation. From her words and actions, we can be privy to a way of life that took a bloody war to destroy. We can also view how tortuous a process it was for Southern whites to accept defeat and to rebuild and recover from the whirlwind of that war.

MARY BOYKIN CHESNUT

Portrait of Mary Boykin Chesnut painted by Samuel Osgood, 1856. Courtesy of the National Portrait Gallery.

Chapter One

─────────────────○─────────────────

Southern Daughter: "The World Seemed a Place Where One Could Be Very Jolly"

THE WEALTHY BOYKIN FAMILY PLANTATION was nestled near the small, centrally located town of Statesburg, South Carolina. It was there, on a late March day in 1823, that Mary Boykin Miller was welcomed into the world by her parents and grandparents. Mary's mother, still almost a child herself at nineteen, and also named Mary Boykin Miller, represented an old, prominent South Carolina family. Her father, Stephen Decatur Miller, was an influential member of the state's political elite. At the time of Mary's birth, the thirty-four year old Miller was one of South Carolina's state senators.

The world into which Mary Miller was born was a privileged one. Mary's maternal grandparents were wealthy plantation owners in Statesburg. The Boykins, Virginians by descent, had been active in the Revolutionary contest, and succeeded in building quite a large plantation in what was then a rather remote and undeveloped part of the state. It was to their home that Mary's mother went to bear her first child.

Mary's father could not claim the same patrician lineage, but he had taken advantage of opportunities available to young, ambitious men in the post-Revolutionary era. Stephen Miller was born at

3

Waxhaw settlement, near the North Carolina border, in 1788. Of Scots-Irish yeomen descent, Miller's early life in many ways paralleled that of another prominent Waxhaw native, Andrew Jackson. Neither man came from wealth, but each rose above their humble beginnings to attain prominence via the law and a career in politics. Miller, however, did have the benefit of a college education, and graduated from South Carolina College in Columbia in 1808. Almost immediately, he went to read law in Statesburg and Sumter where, after just three years, he was admitted to the bar and took over his mentor's law practice.

Miller married his first wife, Eliza Dick, in 1814. She bore him three sons, but only one lived beyond infancy. It was during the early years of this marriage that Miller began his political career when he was elected to the United States Congress in 1814. Eliza's poor health caused Miller enough concern that he moved her to Washington after a serious illness. Despite Miller's ministrations, Eliza died in 1819, and shortly thereafter, at the conclusion of his House term, Miller went home to South Carolina. It was there that he met, fell in love with, and married Mary Boykin. Miller and his new wife lived with the Boykins until Miller purchased a plantation close to his wife's family homestead. Consequently, Mary Boykin Miller, Stephen Miller's first daughter and first child by his second wife, was reared in an environment surrounded by family and friends, all of whom were members of the South Carolina political and social elite.

Mary's earliest recollections were of her Grandmother Boykin. She recalled years later that "I was with her all days—her Shadow— the oldest grand daughter & named for her—her pet." Although the relationship was short (her grandmother died when Mary was eight), Grandmother Boykin introduced her to the plantation world. She helped her grandmother with the morning chores of feeding the chickens and overseeing the dairy; she accompanied her grandmother when she went to the slave quarters to "measure a shirt or a pair of pantaloons" or to mix up "all manner of physic"; and she learned from her grandmother's black seamstresses how to sew and do fancy needle work. It was a busy life, and Mary had a first hand view of how complex and challenging it was for the plantation mistress to manage a plantation as a profitable business operation.

When Mary was not with her Grandmother Boykin, she was with her parents at their Plane Hill plantation. There, Mary received quite a different education, but one that would serve her well in her teenage and adult years. Because her father was active in politics, their home became a haven for local and state political luminaries. Though only a child of five or six, she undoubtedly overheard the discourses on political philosophy that were bandied around the dinner table or in the library. It was from this that Mary gained her lifelong fascination with politics.

In 1828, Mary's father was elected governor of South Carolina. At that time, the tariff issue dominated all state and national discussions. Stephen Miller had gone on record four years earlier in favor of state's rights, and he was instrumental in the founding of the South Carolina State's Rights Party. Miller firmly supported John C. Calhoun's response to the so-called "Tariff of Abominations," the *South Carolina Exposition and Protest*. Miller, like most South Carolinians, regarded the tariff as a burden on the agricultural interests of the state, imposed for the benefit of the manufacturing enterprises of the North. Many South Carolinians went so far as to question the constitutionality of the tariff and the power of Congress to subsidize Northern business. Calhoun forcefully, though anonymously, argued in the *Exposition and Protest* that South Carolina had the right to declare the federal tax null and void.

In 1830, in the midst of the four-year battle over the tariff and nullification, Miller was elected to the U.S. Senate. There, he would continue to champion state's rights and in particular, South Carolina's right to nullify the tariff. While Miller served as Senator, the state's course would bring it to head-on conflict with President Andrew Jackson. Jackson refused to accept the nullification of the tariff, and threatened to send Federal troops to Charleston to collect the duties forcibly. Henry Clay, already known as the "Great Compromiser," as a result of his work on the Missouri Compromise, entered the fray and succeeded in getting Congress to pass a reduced tariff. Clay's compromise tariff allowed both Jackson and South Carolina to claim victory—and to save face. But South Carolina had the last word, and fired the final salvo in the dispute when it nullified Jackson's Force Bill that authorized Federal troops to be sent into the state.

It was in this environment that Mary first came to know politics. She herself noted much later that "My father was a South Carolina Nullifier—Governor of the state at the time of the N[ullification] row & then U.S. Senator, so I was of necessity a rebel born." Although only a child of seven when the conflict reached a fever pitch, she was exposed to the complex doctrines of state's rights, nullification, and the compact theory of government. She accepted them without question, and they formed the core of her political education until her husband, a moderate Unionist at heart, would come into her life just six years later. Indeed, she would, until well into the 1850s, speak with pride about her "nullifier," or Southern radical state's rightist political heritage.

Miller's career necessarily meant that he was absent from home a great deal. Still, he saw to it that his children—Mary would be joined by a brother, Stephen, in 1825, a sister Catherine, (called Kate) in 1827, and another sister, Sarah, (called Sally) in 1831—all had the benefits of his status and position. When Miller traveled on business, Mary and her siblings could visit their Grandmother Boykin at Mount Pleasant. When he was governor, Miller would have the children join him in Columbia, where once again they would be exposed to the excitement of the state legislature's meetings.

Mary, her brother Stephen, and her sister Kate, did not accompany their father to Washington when he assumed his United States Senate seat. Instead, they stayed in Camden where they began their schooling. Mary's first exposure to education outside the plantation took place at a school run by Miss Stella Phelps, a teacher trained at the prestigious Troy Female Seminary in New York. Mary found Miss Phelps a rather stern and "rigid Presbyterian." This demeanor undoubtedly caused Miss Phelps to be driven to distraction by Mary's youthful restlessness.

While Mary attended Miss Stella's school, her father resigned his Senate seat and returned to South Carolina. Although Miller blamed ill health for his resignation, he remained active in South Carolina politics. By 1833, the state's rights faction had divided over the issue of a test-oath. The test-oath, which had been devised during the debates over the Force Bill, stated that South Carolinians would uphold the Nullification Ordinance at all costs. Miller, once one of the most vocal nullifiers, now found himself a moderate who was willing to omit the test-oath in order to keep unionists in the state mollified—the test-oath also stipulated that those who did not take the oath were ineligible to hold state office. Miller was unable to forge a compromise, and his moderation cost him heavily. Calhoun emerged from the imbroglio as the undisputed leader of the state's rights faction. That result, as much as Miller's claim of health problems, probably convinced him to sell his plantation and move his family to other lands he owned in Mississippi.

As MILLER MADE THE ARRANGEMENTS TO MOVE to Mississippi, he also made plans that would change Mary's life rather dramatically. Miller decided that it was time for her to receive a more rigorous and advanced education. Before he left Plane Hill, Miller took twelve-year-old Mary to Charleston in the spring of 1835 and enrolled her in Madame Ann Marsan Talvande's boarding school.

Among the wealthy, education in the nineteenth century South in many ways paralleled the system that was in operation in the North. All members of the upper class, regardless of geographical region, desired to provide their sons and daughters with the best education money could buy. Governesses and private tutors served their purpose when the children were young; when they reached the age of nine or ten, they attended local academies. Those families with even more means would see to it that their children were sent to private day or boarding schools. After that, young males went on to receive higher education, at a Northern university (South Carolina men overwhelming preferred Princeton), a military academy, such as West Point, or a highly regarded local college, such as South Carolina College in Columbia.

For women in the South, education presented unique opportunities—and constraints. Planters wanted their daughters to receive a well-rounded education that emphasized the classics, history, foreign languages, and art. Most schools and academies also included music and dancing lessons in their curricula, as well as fancy needlework. Southern fathers did encourage their daughters to excel in their studies every bit as much as their sons, but their motivation for encouraging such excellence was different. Women were to be educated to make them more attractive to potential suitors. Indeed, a primary purpose of a Southern girl's education was to give her the opportunity to meet prominent young men of the local elite who would be good marriage prospects. Thus, once their schooling was completed (usually at the age of eighteen or twenty), they were expected to marry. No other occupation was open to them. Even so, the education given the young women of the elite did not train them fully for the practical, domestic duties of a plantation mistress. Consequently, many women entered marriage with some background in the liberal arts, but with little inkling as to how to run an estate.

The school to which Mary was sent was one of the finest boarding schools for young women in the country. Madame Ann Talvande's school was located in facing townhouses on the corner of Tradd and Legare Streets in Charleston. According to Mary, Madame, "the Tyrant of Legare St. was of an excellent French family driven to Charleston . . . [and] driven out of San Domingue by Touissant l'Ouverture," the leader of the 1790s slave revolt that was the most successful in history. "Like all refugees, in all times," Mary wrote later, "she wasted no time in vain regrets, or in thoughts of what was due her by God and man" before the rebellion which ousted the French from control of the colony. Although Mary was quite fond of Madame Talvande—and Madame of Mary—she painted a portrait of a stern and intimidating authority figure: Madame "was quite regal in appearance . . . [and] she had the faculty of inspiring terror and by that power she ruled us absolutely. Until she lost her temper Madame was a charming French woman. . . . She was exceedingly polite and her manners very attractive. For all that—she was a cruel despot."

Madame Talvande's school stressed academics and social graces. Girls studied French (Mary, in fact, became quite fluent in that language) history, rhetoric, the natural sciences, and literature. Music, dancing, and embroidery were also available to the girls at extra cost. Such an education did not come cheaply: a typical school term cost over $500. Miscellaneous expenses for items such as books, theater tickets, music lessons and the like could easily push the comprehensive cost close to $700. Hence, only the wealthy could afford to send their daughters there. Perhaps because of that, enrollment remained small. The number of girls at Madame's hovered between twenty-five and fifty, and their ages ranged from 13 to 18.

Mary herself was aware of the importance of class status at Madame Talvande's; she could see it very much in evidence among her classmates. She noted that the planter's daughters were "models of propriety in dress and in conduct." The "Sea Islanders," those who hailed from the Sea Islands off the coast of South Carolina and Georgia, were "long staple [cotton] heiresses. They were a race apart." Mary's view of them was more apt than she probably knew at the time. Families from the Sea Islands represented the wealthiest segment of the population in both states in terms of the value of their land and their slaveholdings. Mary also noted that a "distinct dialect . . . marked them." This unique mode of speaking was in fact a result of the relative isolation of the Sea Islands. The region had an overwhelming slave majority that succeeded in maintaining their African customs and speech, and this linguistic environment influenced their white masters.

Other boarders included the daughters of St. Domingue planters who were, like Madame Talvande, refugees from the rebellion that lasted until 1804. Mary's classmates were rounded out by the descendants of old Huguenot families who had fled France during the 1680s after Louis XIV revoked the Edict of Nantes, the law which had allowed religious toleration for French Protestants.

There is no question that the young ladies who attended Madame Talvande's school were of a higher social status than the majority of the girls their ages. Yet, even within this privileged environment, some girls were more esteemed than others. Indeed, Mary noted that Madame played favorites: those who attended the school "from the beginning" received the most attention from the "tyrant of Legare Street." "For those who were sent here for a few months, 'to finish,'" Mary went on, Madame "felt very slight responsibility" for their training.

From all accounts, Mary reveled in her time at Madame Talvande's. She described the school as "the very beau ideal of 'select school for young ladies,'" but that "it was a Convent in its seclusion." In fact, "The small door in the wall on Legare St.

suggested a Nunnery." According to Mary, the house actually consisted of "two distinct buildings welded together. The one of brick, which opened on Tradd Street, by a Porte Cochere, must have been a grand establishment in its day; so thick were the walls and so fine the wood carving, not to speak of the sculptured white marble mantle pieces." The connecting building was not quite as imposing an edifice. It was made of brick, and contained "three tiers of piazzas open to breezes from East, South and West." Together, the buildings "formed a U—the two arms of which were our school room and our dining room." Mary's room, on the top floor, contained "windows on three sides" which afforded a perfect view of the Charleston Battery. Twelve girls shared that top floor room, a room which included "wash stands and dressing tables, and [on] one side . . . a Piano." "Bed curtains," according to Mary's later description, "formed of our frocks and petticoats" allowed a "modicum of privacy."

Mary's days of carefree hi-jinx and intensive education were to be briefly interrupted in 1836. Apparently, friends of her father saw the bright young Mary, all of thirteen, walking along the Battery with a male companion. This escort was James Chesnut, Jr., a recent Princeton graduate, who was studying law in the city. Stephen Miller decided Mary needed closer supervision—and chaperoning. Consequently, instead of beginning another school year at Madame's in the fall of 1836, Mary returned with her family to Mississippi after their visit east in the spring of that year.

Mary was gravely disappointed to be taken from Madame Talvande's. She believed that "in some inscrutable way . . . it was a punishment." "I had been gay and contented hitherto," she later wrote, "and knew . . . many people thought that wrong." As if anticipating her lifestyle as an adult, Mary concluded that "being too light hearted gave offense."

The trip to Mississippi was long and arduous. Mary recorded years later that ". . . for four or five weeks I was there pent up in close confinement, with my own family. While I was at school the others had twice before made the trip, and they luxuriated in the details of all the hardships I would have to encounter." The landscape, too, bored her, and made her wonder if the family was actually headed for a land far removed from civilization. "There was nothing to divert the eye but monotonous Pine woods," she wrote dejectedly. What houses the Millers passed were "few and far between, each uglier, barer, squarer, more uninteresting than the last."

Mary's trip to Mississippi exposed her to the frontier-like conditions that existed in the southwestern part of the United States. Mississippi had been admitted to the Union in 1817, but it was still a rather untamed land, with a sizeable Indian population. The plantations which her father had purchased (Mary remembered that he owned three that contained "several hundred . . . slaves") were located in the northern part of the state, about seven miles from Carrollton. The house where they settled differed greatly from the gracious home she had enjoyed in South Carolina. The building was no more than a "log cabin of two rooms—with a couple of clap board lean tos." Despite such primitive accomodations, Mary noted that her family had imposed a little refinement on the rather wild surroundings. They "brought . . . fine linen, [and] silver and china" to "this palatial residence, in which we found six chairs and a pine table." Mary's sense of foreboding was reinforced on several occasions when she was awakened by wolves prowling about the house and baying at the moon.

Mary's "exile" to Mississippi would be of short duration. After Mary attended a dance with her brother Stephen and sister Kate at their school, and attracted a host of admirers, her mother prevailed upon Miller to send her back to Madame Talvande's. Though Mary did not consider herself especially attractive, (she would later admit that she "was never handsome" and that she "wonder[ed] what my *attraction* was for men did fall in love with me wherever I went") she was able, throughout her life, to charm men with her wit, intelligence, and vivacious personality. As her mother knew, Mary's charm would make her an object of courting and flirting wherever she went. It would be better, Mrs. Miller reasoned, to have her courted among the gentry of civilized and cultivated Charleston, rather than the wild men of Mississippi. Consequently, Mary was, as she put it, "packed up—& taken back to Charleston" in the spring of 1837.

Mary would be separated from her family for the entire fall, 1837 term of the school year. Miller, consumed by the desire to wring profits from his cotton crop, decided to stay in Mississippi through the hot "sickly" season. That decision would prove to be a dreadful mistake. Each member of the Miller clan came down with the "fever," probably yellow fever or malaria. Undoubtedly remembering the death of his first wife from similar fevers, Miller decided to send the whole family back to Charleston where they could recuperate in more healthful surroundings.

The return of Mary's mother, brother and sisters to the "City By the Sea" marked the beginning of what Mary called a "delightful life." Her sisters joined her at Madame Talvande's, and her mother took up residence at the Planter's Hotel. Every Friday, Mary and Kate, who were boarders, would return to the Hotel to spend the weekend with their Mother and sister Sally, who was enrolled at Madame's as a day student. On other afternoons, Mary remembered, "Mother invented every manner . . . of excuse to come & see us—& to take us out walking with her."

Mary's return to Charleston also marked the rekindling of the romance she had begun with James Chesnut. At the time of Mary's readmission to Madame Talvande's, Chesnut was reading law in the offices of the prominent South Carolina attorney and politician James L. Petigru. Chesnut, at 23, was one of the city's most eligible bachelors; Mary was still a teenager of 15.

James Chesnut came from a distinguished South Carolina family whose status rivalled that of Mary's. Born in 1815 at Camden, South Carolina, to James and Mary Cox Chesnut, he was the youngest of thirteen children. James, like Mary, had all the advantages that growing up as a member of the plantation elite afforded. He was educated at the finest academies and graduated from Princeton University in 1835. Although he was the youngest son, and thus not in line to inherit the vast Chesnut holdings, James, was, nonetheless a cultured, educated, and refined young man, a man fully imbued with the ideals of the Southern white elite.

The courtship of Mary and James continued to blossom under the watchful eye of Mary's mother, who assumed the role of chaperone. Mary recalled years later one such event Mrs. Miller wound up escorting: "[A]s soon as we [her classmates at Madame Talvande's] were all seated in solid phalanx [at a theatre]," Mary reported, "some nice young man who had considerately gone for Mother & persuaded her to come too" appeared. Apparently, James would also ask "Mad T . . . to allow myself & my sister to sit with our Mother. . . . [Mr. Chesnut's] attention to Mother was lovely—& in that way saw him often—& looked on him as sort of a half holiday." Mary concluded her reminiscence with a rhetorical question: "Could any man want to be any thing more delightful to a school girl"?

These happy days were halted tragically in March, 1838, when Mary and her family received word that Stephen Miller had died suddenly at his nephew's plantation in Mississippi. Apparently, Miller succumbed to the fever which had prompted him to send the rest of the family back to Charleston. Mary and her mother, who was herself only thirty-four, found themselves responsible for settling all the affairs in Mississippi. Consequently, mother and daughter journeyed back to Mississippi to sell the lands and slaves there. It was, undoubtedly, a very difficult trip. The Millers stopped first in Alabama, where Mrs. Miller's brother, Francis Boykin, lived. They enlisted the help of the Boykins in dealing with the lengthy—and difficult—negotiations which followed. It became plain after just a short time that Miller's lands were heavily mortgaged. As a result, it took Mary's uncles and her mother months to settle the claims against the land and the Miller estate. The final sale of Stephen Miller's holdings came in June, 1839, almost a year after Miller's death and several months after Mary and her mother had left Mississippi to return to Charleston.

The death of Mary's father had, of necessity, interrupted the romance between James and Mary. James, however, had remained faithful, despite the lengthy separations. In fact, he had sent Mary on her sad journey with a heartfelt love poem he had penned himself. Later, he sent Mary another note in which he first broached the subject of marriage. Mary was not allowed to read the letter and was instructed by her mother and aunts to return it to James with a curt "no." She later recalled that once in Mississippi "I received a letter from Mr C of the most decided kind—quite grateful *at not* being refused." Apparently, Mary had followed her own desires instead of the instructions of her elders, and had not unequivocally turned down James' proposal. She noted, however, that her actions caused "a row—they accused me of not being candid." Mary's aunt wrote the next letter to James, but once again, Mary had the last word. She edited part of the note to soften its originally harsh and discouraging tone.

Evidently, Mary's emendation of the letter served its purpose. Upon her return to South Carolina she again met up with James. But their hopes for marriage were dashed once more. James's brother John, fifteen years James's senior and the heir to the Chesnut plantations, was terribly ill. The Chesnuts decided that it was in John's best interest to go abroad to seek treatment from the best of Europe's doctors. Accordingly, James and John left for a six-month sojourn on the continent. Before he left, however, James wrote Mary another impassioned love letter, and included with it "a diamond ring, which I ask you to accept and to wear. I promise to ask you to accept nothing more for six long months, therefore do receive it & wear it for me."

Mary did not wear the ring at home in Camden, but she did finally tell a friend that she would wear it when she visited the resorts and springs that wealthy South Carolinians flocked to in order to avoid the summer heat. Mary also tried to be a dutiful daughter-in-law-to-be. Just after James and John left, she visited James's family quite frequently. But over time, the worry and fears about the severity of John's illness cast a pall over Mulberry, the Chesnut plantation—a pall Mary found stifling. Her visits to Mulberry became less and less frequent.

The Chesnuts' most fervent hopes and worst fears played themselves out in the fall and winter of 1839. John's health slowly deteriorated in spite of his European doctors. He and James finally decided to return to the United States to try their luck with physicians in New York and Philadelphia. Those doctors were also unable to reverse John's deteriorating condition, and he died in December, 1839.

John's death had profound implications for James—and Mary. John, as eldest, had been trained, almost from birth, to take over the family fortune in land and slaves. James, as youngest son, had followed the career path deemed proper for other sons: private school, university education, and the study of some profession (in James's case, the law). He had, throughout his childhood, adolescence, and young adulthood, been inculcated with the traditions of

Mary Boykin Chesnut. From a carte de visite taken in the 1850s. Courtesy of the South Caroliniana Library, University of South Carolina.

Southern gentlemen. He was, above all, to do his duty, and to maintain the highest moral and ethical standards. Occasionally, James's parents would inform him that he had fallen short of those lofty goals, but on the whole, his life, up to the age of 25, had been marked by that conditioning. Now, as the only surviving son, it was his duty to shift his focus, to learn plantation management and its host of responsibilities. He would, in essence, be required to add master and manager to his profession as attorney.

John's death also affected Mary. It meant that once again, marriage would have to be postponed until a suitable period of mourning had been observed. It also meant that she would enter the Chesnut family as the wife of the heir apparent.

Mary and James were finally married on April 23, 1840, at the Boykin family home, Mount Pleasant. Mary had just turned seventeen, a young bride even in the nineteenth-century South. Her wedding was small—only fifty people attended since the family was still in mourning—but it was fully in keeping with local wedding traditions. As Mary noted later, marriages in the South rarely took place in a church because the churches were too far removed from the planters' homes. Instead, the bride's family used their plantation. Mary also recalled that she and James did not leave after the ceremony. "After the ceremony came music and dancing—and a mighty supper. I use this word advisedly," Mary wrote, "for its proportions were gigantic." The merry-making continued after the sumptuous reception with a series of "uninterrupted dinner parties and balls." "[T]here was no wedding trip—no honeymoon—so to speak, but what could be snatched from a crowd, a gathering of all the families on both sides."

Mary's marriage to James marked the end of her childhood. The freedom that accompanied courtship and adolescence largely vanished once a young woman decided who and when to marry. The happy, carefree periods of parties and cotillions, of flirting and dreaming, were traded for the responsibilities of being a wife. Mary's transition from young girl to plantation mistress would not be accomplished without stress. Indeed, her marriage to James would open another, and often times not entirely happy, chapter of her young life.

Chapter Two

---◯---

Marriage and Politics:
"I Take This Somnolent
Life Coolly"

JAMES CHESNUT TOOK HIS NEW BRIDE to his family's plantation, Mulberry, after their April wedding. Located just a few miles south of Camden, Mulberry had been the Chesnut family home since 1820, but the family had owned the lands comprising the plantation since the previous century. The original owner, John Chesnut, died in 1818, and left the estate to his son, Colonel James Chesnut, Sr., Mary's father-in-law. Colonel Chesnut oversaw the completion of the plantation house, and used Mulberry as his "winter" home from 1820 until 1862.

Mulberry was an imposing three-story mansion overlooking the Wateree River. According to a granddaughter of Colonel Chesnut, the "exterior of the house [was] simple and unadorned, substantial and massive, with walls of brick, roof of slate and steps of marble." The first floor contained most of the rooms used for entertaining and relaxing, including the drawing room, library, and dining room. Mrs. Chesnut's bedroom and the nursery (which doubled as a sewing room) were also located on the first level. The second and third floors each contained six bedrooms which were used for family and guests. Mulberry's basement was divided into storerooms of various kinds, and also housed a wine cellar that stored numerous rare vintages.

Like so many plantations, Mulberry was laid out with an eye to both utility and aesthetic beauty. A "Scotch gardener" had planted an "avenue of live-oaks" up to the house itself. Paved paths "bordered by lilacs and roses" connected the manor house with the kitchen, smokehouse, dairy, and icehouse. Northeast of the house was a large flower garden, strawberry and raspberry patches, and groves of fruit trees. Stables and barns, as well as a wheelwright's shop, cotton gin, and blacksmith's shop, rounded off the estate. Scattered among these dependencies were the far less grand slave quarters. Mulberry was virtually self-sufficient, but whatever supplies could not be gleaned from the plantation could be obtained via the Wateree River. The plantation's boat carried Colonel Chesnut's cotton to his factor in Charleston. The boat would return laden with various items of European or northern import. The boats that plied Mulberry's cotton would be replaced, in 1848, by the railroad which finally linked Camden with Charleston.

Mulberry plantation was a highly successful operation. Mary's journals indicate that the Chesnuts grew cotton, as well as vegetables, beef, poultry, and other livestock. The Wateree River also supplied Mulberry with a supply of fresh fish. Although James's niece later wrote that "There was no ostentatious display at Mulberry in furniture or in table," accounts of holiday festivities indicate otherwise. A typical Christmas dinner consisted of calf's-head soup, turkey, duck, partridges, ham, vegetables, plum pudding, mince pies, jellies and fruits, all washed down with a plentiful supply of champagne from Colonel Chesnut's wine cellars.

Mulberry was not the Chesnuts' only plantation. Colonel Chesnut also owned and operated several neighboring estates, as well as a summer home at Sandy Hill. At these plantations, too, the Colonel raised cotton, corn, and livestock, and oversaw the operation of grist mills, saw mills, and tanneries. The patriarch of the Chesnut clan continued to visit his holdings well into his old age.

Photographs and family memories of Mulberry indicate that it resembled the plantations of Southern legend. Its very size indicated that the Chesnut clan was one of great wealth and prominence. At one time consisting of almost five square miles, Mulberry depended upon a slave labor force of over 500 to cultivate its cotton, grow its fruits and vegetables, and tend to its livestock. It is doubtful that all of that acreage, or even the majority of it was planted with cotton, however. Most Southern planters, especially those who suffered from the depressions of the 1820s and 1830s, consciously strove for self-sufficiency. They also kept large tracts uncultivated as a guard against soil exhaustion. One prominent South Carolina planter, for example, owned over 5,500 acres, but he cultivated cotton on only 750 acres.

The Chesnut wealth seems to have weathered the severe economic depression that gripped South Carolina off and on from 1819 until the early 1840s. Soil erosion, severe drought, the oversupply of cotton which caused prices to plummet—all these factors exacerbated the economic downturn of those years. The arrival of the railroad to the upcountry in the late 1840s helped fall-line towns such as Camden and its hinterland recover from the depressed times, but many once prominent families were unable to survive the long years before prosperity returned.

MARY'S ARRIVAL AT MULBERRY USHERED in a new era in her young life. She was now a wife, and it was a role quite different from anything she had ever assumed before. Gone forever were her days as a carefree, courted Southern belle (though she would continue to be quite a flirt, much to her husband's dismay). Now she would have to be the helpmate, which required that she place all of her husband's desires and concerns ahead of her own. This would not be accomplished without a great deal of effort—and resistance.

Mary did not become a wife without a good bit of education. Advice books and newspaper columns abounded at the time, and helped fill in the gaps left by her more classical education. Nineteenth-century parents were not shy about instructing their daughters in the intricacies of what their new responsibilities entailed. A father's letter to his newlywed daughter in 1835, reprinted in the *Southern Literary Messenger,* was typical of the era—and the advice offered. The writer believed, as did most people of the time, that "A difference with your husband ought to be considered the greatest calamity." Similarly, the local *Camden Journal* freely dispensed wisdom to young women and brides-to-be. It told women that "Men grow sated of beauty, tired of music, are often wearied of conversation, however intelligent, but they can always appreciate a well swept hearth and smiling comfort." The *Journal* also cautioned wives to "always obtain information from [your husband], especially before company, though you may pass yourself as a simpleton. . . . Never forget that a wife owes all her importance to that of her husband. Leave him entirely master of his own actions." Throughout the course of their lives, Southern women were taught to be submissive and genteel. They were also instructed repeatedly that their sole function was to make their husbands happy.

Despite advice books, parental exhortations, and a protracted courtship period, marriage was, for Mary Chesnut, a difficult adjustment. Moving into Mulberry, where she was more a houseguest than a plantation mistress, was only part of the problem. Mary and James were very different personalities with very different tastes and values. As a result, the Chesnut marriage was often strained. Mary wrote candidly after one marital squabble, "After my stormy youth I did so hope for peace and tranquil domestic happiness. There is none for me in this world." Even later, after they had been through many adventures and heartaches together, Mary would note that she still did not really know James:

> Mr. C, thinking himself an open, frank, confiding person, asked me if he *was not*. Truth required me to say that I knew no more what Mr. C thought or felt on any subject now than I did twenty years ago. Sometimes I *feel* that we understand each other a little—then up goes the iron wall once more.

Perhaps because of her relationship with James, Mary reflected on marriage and what it meant throughout her life. Invariably, she jotted down those musings in her journal. One entry, written after she and James had been married over twenty years, is rather sad in its implications for her own life:

> It is only in books that people fall in love with their wives. . . . After all, is it not as with any other copartnership, say traveling

Mulberry Plantation, front elevation. Courtesy of Mrs. John H. Daniels, Camden, South Carolina.

companions? Their future opinion of each other, 'the happiness of the association,' depends entirely on what they really are, not what they felt or thought about each other before they had any possible way of acquiring accurate information as to character, habits, &tc. Love makes it worse.

More striking still was Mary's comparison of marriage with slavery. She was horrified one afternoon to stumble upon a slave auction where a mulatto woman was on the block. Though she noted that her "very soul sickened" at the sight, because it was "too dreadful," Mary went on "to reason—this is not worse than the willing sale most women make of themselves in marriage—nor can the consequences be worse. The Bible authorizes marriage & slavery—poor women! poor slaves!" Mary would never really change her opinions of the marriage bond. But over time, her relationship with James would improve and they would end their days with an affectionate, companionate marriage.

MARY AND JAMES MOVED INTO AN ESTABLISHED plantation unit that already contained a master and mistress—James's parents, Colonel James Chesnut, Sr. and Mary Cox Chesnut. Mulberry was also the home of James's two older sisters. Thus, one of the roles Mary had been reared to assume, that of plantation mistress, was largely taken from her before she even arrived at Mulberry. Not only did old Mrs. Chesnut handle the daily chores and direct the servants, but she had her own daughters to help her with other tasks. As one relative remembered, by the time everyone—including Mary—awakened in the morning, the house had been cleaned, the servants instructed as to their duties for the day, and the meals planned. Mary's only real duty was rising in the morning; her major decisions seemed to be confined to choosing from the array of items that were warming on the breakfast buffet in the dining room.

Mary's new in-laws were strong individuals who possessed almost forbidding personalities. Colonel Chesnut, who had attended Princeton, inherited Mulberry and the Chesnut fortune upon his father's death. Mary believed that Colonel Chesnut was "kind and amiable when not crossed. Given to hospitality on a grand scale. Jovial, genial, friendly, courtly in his politeness." Still, the Colonel had his moments: he ruled Mulberry and his family "As absolute a tyrant as the czar of Russia, the Khan of Tartary—or the sultan of Turkey." He was, to Mary and to others, quite an imposing, not to mention imperious, figure. "He don't believe anybody—he don't trust anybody," Mary wrote later. "He roars and shouts if a pebble of an obstacle is put in his way." When angry, the old colonel was "brusque, sneering, snarling, utterly unbearable. . . ."

Mary Cox Chesnut was opposite in temperament from her husband. She had been born and reared in splendor at Bloomsbury, the Cox estate near Trenton, New Jersey. Her family was one of the oldest and wealthiest in Philadelphia, and had entertained all the leading figures of the Revolutionary generation—including the Marquis de Lafayette and George Washington. Mrs. Chesnut often recounted the time she personally had greeted Washington before he journeyed to New York for his inauguration and considered it the highlight of her life. Mary regarded Mrs. Chesnut, because of her upbringing, as the essence of a lady—one who demanded similar behavior from her own family. "When anyone here transgresses some plain rule of good breeding," Mary remembered, Mrs. Chesnut's "mild rebuke [was] 'Ah, you were not brought up at Bloomsbury.'"

Mrs. Chesnut and Mary seem to have had a rather tense relationship. In some ways, this was not surprising; they were both strong, independent-minded women. According to Mary, the matriarch of the Chesnut clan never harbored "evil thoughts" about others, and never tolerated gossip from anyone, especially someone living under her roof. It often seemed as if she shamed those around her into proper behavior because she herself was so above reproach. "[Old] Mrs. Chesnut," Mary recalled, "set her face resolutely to see only the pleasant things of life and shut her eyes to wrong and said it was not there. . . . She sat like a canary bird in her nest, with no care or thought of tomorrow." Because of her station in life, Mrs. Chesnut did not have to worry about the morrow: "She lived in a physical paradise and made her atmosphere a roseate-hued mist for her own private delusion."

Mary's mother-in-law also seemed to dissociate herself from all things Southern. Indeed, despite living in the South for almost fifty years, she never really became accustomed to the unique features of the region. Mary noted for example that her mother-in-law had little taste for Southern cuisine: "She cannot like hominy for breakfast and rice for dinner without a relish to give it some flavor. She cannot eat watermelon and sweet potatoes sans discretion as we do." Mary also believed that "Mrs. Chesnut, ever since she came here sixty or seventy years ago as a bride from Philadelphia, has been trying to make it up to the negroes for being slaves." Still, Mrs. Chesnut possessed certain virtues that Mary respected enormously: she had "a talent for organizing, training [servants], making things comfortable and to move without noise. . . ." Moreover, she loved to read as much as her daughter-in-law. She was, Mary recorded, "The most devoted, unremitting reader of fiction I ever knew"—and had the uncanny knack of obtaining every new book or magazine as soon as it appeared in print.

Given such talents on the part of the plantation mistress and the presence of numerous slaves, it was no wonder that Mary led a rather purposeless and empty life as a bride. To be sure, Mrs. Chesnut would put Mary and her daughters to work sewing clothes for the slave children, and would take the girls with her when she went to the slave quarters to minister to their illnesses. But those activities only took up so much time in a given day. Consequently, Mary came to relish stealing away to her room on the top floor of Mulberry. There, she would read, write, and take in the sights of the plantation.

Mary's retreat was a big "airy" room that had large windows and "deep window seats." There, she could watch the comings and goings of various members of the Chesnut clan and their visitors, who seemed to be a permanent fixture at Mulberry. Mary would note that "The house is crammed from garret to cellar without intermission." At other times, Mary preferred to "sit here in the library alone." She read voraciously anything and everything she could get. Mary's favorite books were novels (a type of literature she had seldom been allowed to read while enrolled at Madame Talvande's), and she particularly enjoyed Charles Dickens. Her rigorous education had taught her to peruse as well great works of literature, the Bible, history, and science. She continued to read works in French as well as German. Reading allowed Mary to continue to develop intellectually; it also provided her with an outlet to escape the boredom that invariably crept in. As Mary herself said, "I take this somnolent life coolly. I could sleep upon bare boards if I could once more be amidst the stir and excitement of a live world. These people," Mary recorded with pen dipped in acid, "have grown accustomed to dullness. They were born and bred in it. They like it as well as anything else."

Mary also used her bedroom retreat to write in day books. She would copy into them bits of Scripture and sermons she had heard on a particular Sunday. Or she would record the daily goings-on at Mulberry. These day books would evolve, in less than twenty years, into the journals she kept during the Civil War years.

Mulberry Plantation, side elevation. Courtesy of Mrs. John H. Daniels, Camden, South Carolina.

When Mary had the chance, she would ride into Camden to visit her mother and sisters, or to browse in some of the small shops that lined the shaded streets. But Camden did not exactly represent the "stir and excitement" Mary would have liked. Camden, in the early 1840s was a prosperous, growing commercial town. Still, it lagged well behind Charleston or Columbia in terms of sophistication. One visitor wrote that Camden "had a quaint look, with its dingy frame buildings and sandy streets." The town's sidewalks were "fringed with grass which was a receptacle for cigar stumps and trash. . . . Hogs, horses and cows roamed at will through the streets." When she could arrange it, Mary would journey to the more "civilized" cities of Columbia and Charleston. For the most part, however, she remained at Mulberry leading what she called a "pleasant, empty, easygoing life. If one's heart is at ease." But Mary's heart was not "at ease" during those years. "[P]eople are not like pigs," she wrote at one point. "[T]hey cannot be put up and fattened. So here I pine and fret."

IN SOME WAYS, JAMES CHESNUT, too, led a rather superfluous existence at Mulberry. To be sure, one day he would take over the management of the plantation, but his father, at sixty-seven, was in good health. Consequently, James continued his law career and would use that as a springboard to state politics. James could have allowed his status as heir apparent to lull him into lugubrious inactivity, but he did not. He had opportunities outside of Mulberry—opportunities that Mary, as a woman, lacked. Thus, he could escape the "somnolent" routine that so often bored his vivacious young wife.

The year of their marriage was also the year James began a political career that would span almost four decades. In 1840, James was elected to the South Carolina General Assembly. With the exception of two terms, the 1846–47 session, and the 1848–49 session, he served continuously in the lower house until 1852. While he was on state business in Columbia or elsewhere, Mary remained at home at Mulberry.

In a sense, James's decision to enter politics was fully in keeping with his status as a younger son, even though he was now destined to be the heir of the Chesnut fortune. Antebellum Southern politics were designed to aid second or third sons. Although primogeniture was not the law as it was in Europe, many Southern families continued to follow the tradition of bequeathing the entire estate to the first born son. By entrusting the family fortune and estate to the eldest son, Southerners believed that they would better preserve the family's status and honor. Those not in line to inherit the family plantation had to choose other areas in which to make their mark. Most second and third sons followed career paths in either the military, the law, or the ministry.

A political career allowed those not destined to take conrol of the family estate an opportunity to lay claim to their own unique place in Southern society. The politics of that era reinforced such trends. They exhibited what one scholar has termed a "familial closed character." Kin relations were crucial to being elected and maintaining political office, especially in a state that valued tradition and rule by the "better sort" as much as South Carolina. In fact, most Southerners viewed elections as serving a dual purpose: they benefited the community and they validated one's personal and more importantly, one's family honor and prestige.

Although politics represented an alternative career path for younger sons, there seemed to be an unspoken assumption that those sons would eventually become planters in their own right and by their own means (via marriage or the profits from a successful law practice). This was especially the case in antebellum South Carolina, where the plantation elite dominated all state and national offices. Indeed, most men who entered politics over time amassed the means to acquire land and slaves, and thus additional cachet in social and political circles. As a result, the state's political leadership was composed primarily of a hyphenated class, the planter-politician.

James's decision not to run in 1846 after serving successfully for several years in the state house may have been prompted by Mary's poor health. In 1845 she became quite ill, perhaps the result of a miscarriage, and her doctors decided that she should travel north to the healing waters of Saratoga Springs, New York, or to the resorts of Newport, Rhode Island. James's sister, Emma, who was slowly dying of tuberculosis, joined the couple on their trip. Evidently, Mary recovered quite quickly once they steamed away from Charleston. Emma wrote to her father back at Mulberry that the rough seas of the Atlantic made everyone "with the single exception of Mary" seasick. Emma also noted that James and Mary kept quite busy, another indication that Mary was recuperating at a rapid pace. Obviously, the change away from Mulberry did her good. Emma reported some time later that "It is impossible to tell you how much Mary has improved, it is really wonderful. She was not at all sea sick, went to every meal & laughed & talked with any body that was well enough to join her."

Though Mary seemed to improve after her visit to Newport, subsequent events indicate that her recovery was limited. Indeed, the persistence of her medical problems prompted Mary and James to decide on the spur of the moment to sail for England. This news surprised the elder Chesnuts. Colonel Chesnut wrote to James in late August, 1845: "Your determination to sail for London was so unexpected to us & I expect, so sudden that you have not prepared yourself with letters of credit or introduction which might become necessary, should sickness or protracted stay or any other cause render them necessary." Mrs. Chesnut, too, voiced concern at the news that Mary and James had sailed off without warning and without adequate funds and letters. She wrote that she and Mary's mother had been quite worried, but reasoned that "if Mary was not as well as you expected after trying the Bathing then it was the best thing you could have done."

Colonel Chesnut did see to it that his son and daughter-in-law were sent the proper letters of credit and introduction. In fact, Secretary of State James Buchanan wrote to American ambassador in England Louis McLane that James and "his lady" had journeyed to London "in pursuance of medical advice." A subsequent letter from Mrs. Chesnut seems to indicate that Mary's medical problems were still related to miscarriages.

Despite ill health, Mary thoroughly enjoyed her trips to the fashionable summer residences of the elite in New York and Rhode Island and to London. She and James were able to indulge in their favorite hobby, buying books, and Mary was able to taste some of the excitement and social whirl that she missed at Mulberry. Upon their return to the United States, Mary managed to visit James's relatives in Philadelphia and Trenton, and there she was exposed, yet again, to the cultivated world of the Northern upper class. Captivated by these visits, she tried every year thereafter to travel, either north to relatives, or to the fashionable springs of Saratoga and Virginia, to satisfy her appetite for shopping, visiting, and socializing.

Mary's poor health may have improved after her protracted travels, but she would be sick again in 1848—the only other time James did not seek re-election to the South Carolina General Assembly. Once again, Mary and James departed for Saratoga, but they got no farther than Philadelphia where they stayed for more medical advice. There is no clear indication of what Mary's ailments were throughout this period, but evidence suggests she was still having problems with pregnancy and miscarriages. She and James remained in Philadelphia until early fall, at which time they returned to Camden.

Upon their return, James purchased a house in the town of Camden. It bore the poetic name "Frogvale," and they happily set up housekeeping. For the first time in her eight years of marriage, Mary had her own home; she could finally be the mistress of the household.

Mary did not waste any time in assuming her domestic duties, throwing herself into them with enthusiasm. This activity, not to mention the realization that she would finally fulfill at least a part of her proper function in life, helped to melt away a good bit of the depression she had suffered during the past several years. Most of this depression had been caused by the dawning realization that she and James would never be able to have children.

The failure of a woman to bear children in the antebellum South had far-reaching consequences. According to the values of the time, no woman was considered "complete" unless she bore her husband several children. Because most women married young, they spent most of their married lives in various stages of pregnancy. Mary's mother-in-law, for example, gave birth to thirteen children, though only four survived to adulthood. Mary's own mother had four children before she was widowed at the young age of thirty-four. If a woman was unable to have children, she was considered a failure in fulfilling her role as a life-giver, a nurturer of the young, and provider of a family heir. Consequently, society considered childless women as "contemptible or at best pitiable."

Mary was well aware of society's views. In fact, she had only to listen to her in-laws to realize that she was somehow inadequate, something less than a full woman. Colonel Chesnut would all too frequently talk and brag about all the children Mrs. Chesnut had given him. According to the Colonel, his wife had not been "useless" because she had produced numerous sons and daughters. Mary could not remain oblivious to such comments. She recorded in her day books on more than one occasion her feelings of inadequacy because of her "barrenness": "God help me—no good have I done—

to myself or anyone else." Her language is instructive: she perceived herself as having little worth because she had not had children to carry on the Chesnut name. This reality would haunt Mary throughout her life.

Despite the fact that she would never have her own family, Mary always enjoyed the company of children, and for most of her life, she would have young people around her or living under her roof. James had numerous nieces and nephews who often came to visit them at Frogvale. Moreover, Mary's favorite sister Kate, who married James's nephew David Williams in 1846, would eventually have five children of her own. Kate's children would visit Mary quite frequently. They adored their "Aunty," and Mary returned the sentiment, calling Kate and David's children her "sweet Williams."

The visit of young relatives helped Mary dispell her nagging sense of loss. The continued course of James's political career also enabled Mary to cope with her bouts of depression and to place her energies in other, more constructive channels. Given her education and her childhood socialization into state politics, it was natural that Mary would take an active interest and role in James's political affairs. Like other educated and intelligent women, she would be an important part of the political culture of the time even though she had no direct voice in it. Though women were disfranchised until the twentieth century, they still played a significant and visible role, assisting their husbands or participating in reform movements. Hence, it was almost natural that Mary Chesnut would become, over time, one of James's chief political aides.

JAMES CONTINUED TO PLAY A PROMINENT and influential role in South Carolina politics during a period of increasing sectional tension. In many ways, he was an ideal politician for the state, for his family was a long standing member of the plantation elite. More than any other Southern state, South Carolina maintained a deferential, oligarchic system that favored the low country plantation interests over the upcountry. The state had, for the most part, withstood the political reforms that swept the country in the 1830s and 1840s. South Carolina's leaders had grudgingly allowed the institution of universal suffrage for white males in 1808, but they saw no reason to go any farther. Even with this democratic reform, voters had little direct influence on the system. In fact, many offices remained appointive.

Throughout the colonial and early national period, South Carolina's planter elite was also the political elite, and it dominated all state and national contests for office. The spread of the cotton kingdom to the upcountry early in the nineteenth century helped to chip away at the lowcountry's dominance of society and government, and especially Charleston's disproportionate influence in state politics. But the early boom in cotton in the upcountry produced a class of leaders little different in ideology or temperament from their low country counterparts. They, too, were wealthy planters who were united in their desire to protect the interests of South Carolina.

As part of that political elite, James became embroiled in the state's debates over the Mexican War and the Wilmot Proviso in late 1849 and 1850. American settlers in Texas had declared themselves independent of Mexico in 1836, but they were unsuccessful in getting President Jackson to recognize their independence, let alone their push for statehood. Consequently, Texas remained an independent republic until 1844, when the whole Texas question became a hot political issue in the presidential contest of that year. A dark horse Democratic candidate, James K. Polk of Tennessee, was elected president on a platform pledging to annex Texas. Following the election, Congress in early 1845 accomplished the annexation by a joint congressional resolution. The annexation, however, did not resolve a dispute between Texas and Mexico over the border. The dispute escalated into war between the United States and Mexico in 1846.

The Mexican War was a very divisive one because it stirred up the controversy over the extension of slavery into the western territories. Northerners feared the results of the war, for it extended the possibility that any lands gained from Mexico could be opened to slavery. To guard against this possibility, Representative David Wilmot of Pennsylvania in August, 1846, proposed an amendment to a war appropriations bill that would have banned slavery from all territory obtained from Mexico after the conclusion of the war. The Wilmot Proviso, as it came to be called, rocked the country: Southerners saw their right to move freely with their property abridged, while Northerners applauded the effort to rein in the "slave power." Although the Proviso passed the House, it was defeated in the Senate. Nonetheless, the damage had been done. The issue of slavery in the territories would now dominate all debates until 1860.

As might be expected, the issue Wilmot raised would resurface in 1848, when the United States and Mexico signed the Treaty of Guadelupe-Hidalgo. In that treaty, Mexico ceded over 500,000 square miles of territory, from Texas to the California coast, to the United States. The situation was explosive because many in Congress believed that a Mexican law forbidding slavery remained in effect in the lands obtained by the treaty. Thereafter, Northerners and Southerners eyed each other warily as they waited to see who the new president would be and what position he would take on the status of the newly acquired territories.

The issue of slavery in western lands became even more important when gold was discovered in California. The news reached the East Coast toward the end of 1848, and the Gold Rush ensued. The influx of over 80,000 people between 1848 and 1849 necessitated that some type of government, territorial or state, be established to effect some order.

This struggle over slavery in the Mexican Cession formed the backdrop to the 1848 presidential contest, and resulted in the election of Whig candidate and Southern war hero Zachary Taylor. Believing that a strong stance could mitigate sectional tensions, Taylor declared in his inaugural address in March and in a speech to Congress in December, 1849, that the states which would be formed out of the Mexican Cession should decide for themselves whether they would have slavery or not. Taylor was convinced that bypassing the territorial stage would remove Congress from the fray and thus eliminate divisive debates over slavery in the territories. He would endorse this policy by recognizing California's request for admission as a free state in late 1849. Taylor also proposed that New Mexico be organized and admitted to the Union under a similar formula. What

Taylor implied in his speech was clear to Southerners: the president was calling for the virtual adoption of the Wilmot Proviso.

Initially, Southerners had greeted Taylor's election with relief. He was, after all, one of Louisiana's largest slaveholders. But Taylor's subsequent pronouncements indicated that he may not have been "safe" on Southern concerns, especially, slavery. Even before Taylor had announced his plan for the Mexican Cession, Southern politicians were busy, pushing for bipartisan unity on Southern issues. The Mississippi Slaveholders' Convention meeting in October, 1849, went one step further, and called for an all-southern convention to meet in Nashville in June, 1850.

The Nashville Convention marked James Chesnut's entry into the regional and ultimately, national political limelight. He was elected as a delegate representing South Carolina at that meeting. But James would be involved in pre-convention caucusings with such state luminaries as James Henry Hammond well before journeying to Nashville. These meetings were designed to map out the state's strategy once the delegation arrived in Nashville. According to Mary, James "represented the conservative and moderate wing of the southern rights party." The irony of that stance could not have been lost on Mary. Her father, after all, had been one of the founders of the state's rights wing of the party, and had been an ardent nullifier in the 1820s and 1830s.

James's preparations for the Nashville Convention coincided with the unfolding of events in the nation's capital. While President Taylor continued to urge that California and New Mexico be admitted as free states, Senator Henry Clay of Kentucky, the "Great Compromiser," became involved. Clay presented his Omnibus Bill to the Senate in February, 1850. This bill, Clay believed, had eight parts that would give something to every section. Included in Clay's Omnibus Bill was the admission of California as a free state, a tougher Fugitive Slave Law, and the abolition of the slave trade in the nation's capital. The issue of the remaining territories of the Mexican Cession was left sufficently ambiguous: they were to be left "without the adoption of any restriction or condition on the subject of slavery." Clay's proposals immediately touched off a debate that saw political and sectional oratory rise to new heights.

John C. Calhoun, old and dying, made his final appearance in the Senate; Daniel Webster argued passionately for Union; and a number of up-and-coming politicians, including William H. Seward, Jefferson Davis, and Stephen A. Douglas, debated the course of the nation's future.

The contest in the Senate raged into June, and thus provided James Chesnut and the other Southern delegates who attended the Nashville Convention a focus for their discussions. Mary watched all these events unfold with great interest, and kept in close correspondence with James over the twists and turns of the political situation. Interestingly, Mary found herself slowly altering the political views she had held since her youth. She wrote to James in Nashville: "I think I am in danger of turning a regular somerset [sic] in *my* politics & transferring my allegiance from Mr. Calhoun right away to Clay—particularly as I am not the *hearty* lover of slavery this latitude requires—in spite of [Calhoun's] appreciation of Southern virtues. . . ." Mary reflected on her new attitude. "I shall not dilate upon the Nashville convention merely to fill up paper—as I am not *sound* on certain important *topics* now so constantly discussed— indeed so very heterodox am I—that I principally *hate* the abolitionists for their *cant* & abuse of us—& worse than all their using this vexed question as a political engine. . . ." She begged James to keep her abreast of all the happenings: "you must *make* time to write me long letters as I am *intensely* curious as to your movements."

Mary's correspondence with James on his activities in Nashville in particular and on the heated issues of 1849–50 in general demonstrate what a solid grasp she had on current events. Though she had been inculcated with the doctrines of nullification and state's rights as a young girl, her careful reading of political speeches, documents, and the like had altered her earlier views. Without doubt, her early education and the environment in which she matured created in her an awareness of political issues and ideologies that other, less privileged women lacked. Throughout her life, Mary would be an interested, enthusiastic, and independent student of politics and political discourse.

In many ways, Mary used James's position and influence to satisfy her own longings for an active life and career outside the home. With servants to maintain the daily routine at Frogvale, and with no children to monopolize her time, Mary increasingly took an avid interest in all James did. Before too long, she would become his personal secretary. Perhaps even more than her intelligent and informed letters to her husband, her service as secretary demonstrates both her ability and the trust James had in those abilities.

The men who convened in Nashville did not represent the entire South as Calhoun and the other planners had hoped. James and his colleagues from South Carolina comprised the fullest delegation present in Tennessee's capital city. They and the other Southern delegates who attended the convention quickly found themselves somewhat divided and adrift. The goal of the convention had been to reaffirm the need to protect Southern rights and to develop a plan to prevent the admission of California as a free state. But once they met, the delegates discovered that they disagreed as to the best means of achieving their goals. They also found that by the time they convened in 1850, Clay's bill was the subject of national debate. As a result, the delegates to the Nashville Convention put their discussions on hold until the Senate decided on Clay's package. The convention did issue a series of resolutions calling for the recognition of Southern rights and resolved to meet again should the situation demand it. After adopting that futile but face-saving measure, the convention adjourned.

The crisis over the future of the Mexican Cession dragged on well into summer. On the Fourth of July, the nation was shocked to learn that President Taylor had died suddenly after attending a parade in hot, humid Washington. Just a few weeks later, Clay's Omnibus Bill was defeated, and the tired author left Washington exhausted from the months-long debate. Into the fray stepped Senator Stephen Douglas of Illinois. Douglas perceived that Clay's bill had elements that both sections supported, but that it was doomed as an omnibus package. Douglas divided the bill into separate parts (a plan that Clay had originally discussed with a Senate colleague) to try and take advantage of shifting sectional coalitions. The Little Giant was also aided by Taylor's presidential successor, Millard Fillmore, who was much more amenable to Clay's compromise package than Taylor had been. Fillmore's support, coupled with Douglas's shrewd lobbying of crucial swing blocs, succeeded in getting each element through the Congress. Thus, the individual components of Clay's Omnibus Bill were passed, but in a rather ominous fashion: each section voted only for those parts that benefited itself. This became known as the Compromise of 1850. But, as many people then—and now—noted, there was little in the final legislation which indicated that it was, indeed, a compromise. Instead, it was more of an armistice. It allowed each section to claim victory, but it also strengthened the hand of the radical elements in both the North and South.

James returned to Camden after the Nashville Convention, but he did not remain there long. In 1852, largely as a result of the exposure he gained at Nashville and his defense of Southern rights, James was elected to the South Carolina State Senate. He would continue to serve in that capacity, and was from 1856 to 1858, president of the Senate. Perhaps in keeping with his new status, James and Mary sold Frogvale and moved into a larger home in the northern section of Camden known as Kirkwood. The Chesnuts renamed the house "Kamchatka."

Mary would not be able to enjoy her spacious home for long. James's political career became even more demanding after he was elected to the State Senate. Mary continued to serve as his secretary, answering his growing correspondence, and maintained a lively social schedule. But the tide of events was rapidly overtaking Mary and James Chesnut.

In many ways, 1858 marked a turning point for Mary and for South Carolina. In that year, factional divisions within the South Carolina Democratic Party produced a deadlock among several of the leading candidates for one of the state's seats in the United States Senate. James's reputation as a moderate with a commitment to state's rights held him in good stead, and he was elected to the vacant Senate seat. Mary greeted the news with joy, anticipating the exciting social life of the nation's capital. She set about organizing their affairs and obtaining the latest Parisian fashions so she could dress the part of the wife of a U.S. senator. Since life in Washington would be far more expensive than rural South Carolina, Mary and James also sold Kamchatka.

Washington in the late 1850s was a whirl of parties and politics. Mary could not have chosen a better time to take up residence in the nation's capital. Finally, after years of living in the relative backwater of Camden, she would have the opportunity to move in the company of all the leading figures of the day.

The Chesnuts initially set up their household in rented rooms at Brown's Hotel on Pennsylvania Avenue. According to one of her Southern neighbors, Mary was one of the real stand-outs at that "rendezvous of Southern Congressmen." Very quickly, Mary earned a reputation as "an accomplished linguist" because of her facility with French and German. She was also "ranked high among the cultured women of the capital."

Mary plunged into the Washington maelstrom with gusto. She made friends quickly and easily, and soon came to know virtually all the Southern senators and their wives, including Varina Howell Davis, wife of future president of the Confederacy Jefferson Davis. On a typical day, Mary would go calling on friends, attend a luncheon, and perhaps go shopping. The evening hours were devoted to the theatre, lectures, or dinner parties. James often declined invitations, but his reluctance to hobnob with the political elite did not discourage Mary. In fact, she demonstrated her independence by sometimes attending parties without him. Over time, as Mary and James's social engagements became more extensive, Mary found their lodgings at Brown's insufficient. In January, 1860, Mary convinced James to rent a house. They took up residence at H and Tenth Streets, where Mary would have an opportunity to display her talent for throwing lavish dinner parties.

MARY'S CAREFREE LIFE IN THE CAPITAL CITY belied the growing tensions that dominated politics during the late 1850s. When James was elected to the Senate, the nation was still digesting the import of the Supreme Court's 1857 decision in *Dred Scott v. Sanford*. The high court ruled that Dred Scott, a slave who had been taken to free territory, remained a slave and that Congress could not prohibit slavery in the territories. That landmark decision, which Chief Justice Roger B. Taney hoped would settle the slavery issue once and for all, served only to inflame the situation.

One unanticipated result of the *Dred Scott* decision was the dramatic growth of the Republican Party. Born in 1854 as a result of the Kansas–Nebraska Act, the party was pledged to a platform of "free soil, free labor, and free men." The Republicans were a purely sectional party, and their stance frightened and infuriated Southerners. The Republicans' successes in the 1858 midterm elections portended a heated presidential contest in 1860.

Given the atmosphere, Mary and James could not help but discuss the pressing issues of the day, including slavery. In the Senate, James was accorded a great deal of respect because of his reasoned, eloquent oratory in defense of slavery. He responded to a colleague's speech condemning slavery in the western territories by noting that "Commerce, civilization, and Christianity go hand in hand and their conjoint efforts receive their earthly impulse from this . . . institution [of slavery]."

Mary, in a show of her intellectual independence, however, did not hold the same views as her husband. In fact, she wrote often about the evils of slavery. One such entry in her journal mused : "I wonder if it be a sin to think slavery a curse to any land. [Senator Charles] Sumner said not one word of this hated institution [in his famous speech] which is not true. . . . God forgive *us*, but ours is a *monstrous* system & wrong & iniquity." Mary recorded sometime later that she had found a letter she had written to James in 1842. "It is," she noted, "the most fervid abolition document I have ever read." She admitted she had burned other letters, but not that one. "I kept it—as showing how we are not as much heathens down here as our enlightened enemies think."

Mary's comment about the abolitionist nature of her letter is, at first glance, striking. She would continue to rail against slavery and its effect on the South throughout the region's march toward secession and war. Yet, she was not, in any meaningful way, a true abolitionist. Mary could vent her frustrations about slavery and slaveholders to her husband and others, but at bottom, she was committed to the institution—and totally dependent upon it. Mary Chesnut could not have enjoyed the life she did from birth until well into adulthood without the aid of her family's slaves. Indeed, from the time she awoke, throughout her day, as she entertained, even as she prepared for bed, she was surrounded by and attended to by slaves. Mary could live a life of ease only because of the institution she supposedly loathed. She could afford the luxury of thinking about slavery and condemning it only because the slaves who worked for her gave her that leisure.

The passing of time did not defuse the slavery issue, nor lessen the tension between North and South. In the following year, 1859, tensions reached an even higher pitch. The event that forced renewed recriminations was John Brown's attempt in October of that year to start a slave uprising by seizing the federal arsenal at Harpers Ferry, Virginia. Brown was hanged for treason, but Northern sympathy for his death caused many Southerners to reach the conclusion that they were living in a hostile land. Brown's raid, *Dred Scott*, problems in Kansas—all these events would loom large as the presidential election of 1860 approached. Mary, busy entertaining, attending parties, or traveling to visit relatives, had no inkling as to how dramatically the election of 1860 would alter her life.

Chapter Three

─────────○─────────

1860–1861:
"Lincoln Was Elected
and Our Fate Sealed"

MARY AND JAMES CHESNUT WERE LITTLE DIFFERENT from most Americans in North and South in 1860: they greeted the spring presidential campaigning season with great interest and concern. The debates of the late 1850s had left many with a nagging sense of foreboding. Some hoped that a new administration would settle the territorial issue and implicitly, the slavery issue, once and for all. Others believed that the existence of a truly sectional party, the Republicans, signaled that a peaceful resolution to the conflict was impossible.

By 1860, there was only one national organization left that could claim to have branches in both North and South: the Democratic Party. The major Protestant religious denominations, other clubs and organizations—all had broken into Northern and Southern components. Even the railroads, rapidly becoming the nation's prime means of freight transportation, ran on different gauges of track in the two sections. Consequently, there was a good bit of attention attached to the April Democratic National Convention and how it would react to the nation's continued division into sectional components.

For some reason, the Democrats chose the worst possible location for their convention: Charleston, South Carolina. Moderate, reasoned debate hardly stood a chance, with a meeting in the cradle of nullification. Even the weather refused to cooperate, as unseasonably hot and humid air drifted over the city. Nonetheless, the party leadership hoped to unite the warring factions of the party.

The followers of Stephen Douglas of Illinois controlled the party machinery. They were acutely aware that many members of the party disliked Douglas because of his split with President James Buchanan over the Lecompton Constitution which allowed for slavery in Kansas. Some Democrats hoped that pre-nomination manuevering would create a compromise on the platform that would allow Southern delegates to support both it and Douglas. Those moderates would be frustrated in their attempts to maintain party unity.

Although South Carolinians had earned the reputation for being extremists, it was William Lowndes Yancey of Alabama who played the role of fire-eating agitator at the convention. He demanded in his "Alabama Platform" that the convention adopt as one of the party's planks a call for congressional protection of slavery in the territories. The Northern Democratic delegates—and Douglas— could not endorse such a plan because it would have cost the party votes in the North. Frustrated, Yancey and the Alabama delegation walked out, followed by the delegates from the states of the lower South. They would reconvene on June 11 in Richmond, Virginia, but would not accomplish anything of import.

With the walkout of the Deep South, the Convention lacked the required two-thirds majority needed to nominate a candidate. Consequently, the remaining delegates were forced to adjourn, but not before they resolved to reconvene in another, less emotional setting. By the middle of June, they were meeting in Baltimore.

The divisions between the Democrats that were laid bare at Charleston did not go away with the move to Maryland. Instead, the acrimony continued, and new issues served to whip up emotions even more. Almost immediately, debate raged over whether newly-chosen pro-Douglas delegations from the Deep South should represent those states in the reconstituted convention. When it became apparent that the Douglas-dominated delegations (from Alabama, Louisiana, and Georgia in particular) would be seated, would give Douglas a majority, and almost certainly, the nomination, they acted: those who had walked out at Charleston walked out again. Once they left, the pro-Douglas delegates prevailed, and they pushed through a resolution that declared the Little Giant the Democratic Party's nominee even though he lacked the requisite two-thirds of the original convention.

Those who had bolted for a second time reconvened on June 19 at a different location in Baltimore, where they adopted a platform pledged to protect slavery in the territories. Those delegates then nominated John C. Breckinridge of Kentucky as the standard-bearer of the Southern Democrats. The Democratic Party, the last remaining national organization, was now hopelessly split.

The division among the Democrats encouraged moderates and conservatives from both sections to organize yet a third party, the Constitutional Unionists. That group nominated John Bell of Tennessee on an innocuous platform pledged to preserve the Union.

Republican Party members who convened in Chicago in May of 1860 reacted to the April break up of the Democratic Party with emotions that ranged from confidence to glee. After choosing the relatively obscure Abraham Lincoln of Illinois as their candidate, the Republicans adopted a platform that Southerners could only view with alarm. The plank that enraged them most was one that called for the prohibition of slavery in the territories. Southerners had fought against such a ban for years. The prospect that a sectional party would drive them out of an equal share in the western territories was a threat that could not be tolerated. Also of concern were the Republican platform's economic planks that endorsed a national bank, protective tariff benefiting Northern industries, and federal aid for internal improvements. Southerners had long opposed all of these programs because they smacked of an increase in the central government at the expense of the states.

SOUTH CAROLINIANS WATCHED THE SUMMER and early fall canvass closely. Interestingly, the state was quite divided over the course it—and the rest of the South—should take if a "black Republican" were elected to the presidency. James Chesnut, as one of South Carolina's senators, was particularly apprehensive about the future. Although James had always followed the moderate course in the state's politics, he came out during one session of the Thirty-sixth Congress (March 1859–March 1861) fully in favor of Mississippi Senator Jefferson Davis's call for federal protection of slavery in the territories. Chesnut and his Senate colleague James Henry Hammond frequently discussed what course the state should follow if Lincoln was elected. Chesnut wrote to Hammond that he was coming to the conclusion that South Carolina might have to act unilaterally and secede if the situation warranted. Treading cautiously, he promised that he would not publicly endorse such a position before he "consulted" with Hammond and "other friends."

While these momentous events were unfolding, Mary Chesnut was visiting relatives in Alabama and Florida. Given her interest in politics, she was probably fascinated by all the news, and undoubtedly wrote at length to James about the situation. Unfortunately, her thoughts on the crisis have not been preserved. She began her return trip to South Carolina virtually on the eve of the presidential election. She later recorded that she "heard on the cars returning to the world that Lincoln was elected & our fate sealed." Three days later, on November 10, 1860, James Chesnut resigned his U.S. Senate seat. He was the first Southerner to do so. Mary was, quite literally, stunned. She could not believe that James would undertake so drastic a step and not consult with her first. She also had a difficult time accepting the reality that her busy, grand life in Washington was coming to such an abrupt end. Her comments, recorded in her journal after learning of James's resignation, betrayed her disappointment: "At Kingsville [South Carolina] I met my husband; he had resigned his seat in the Senate . . . & was on his way home. Had burned his ships behind him. No hope now—he was in bitter earnest." Mary conceded that she "thought him right" in his decision, but added that "going back to Mulberry to live was indeed offering up my life on the alter of country."

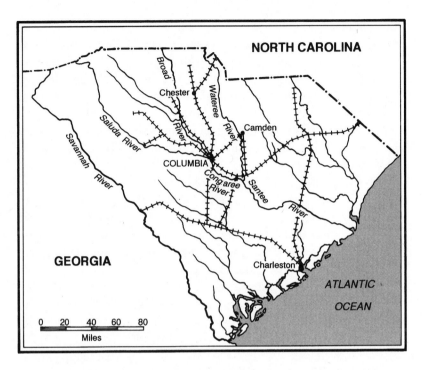

This map of South Carolina in 1860 shows the importance of railroad transportation in the antebellum South.

Mary and James journeyed back to Camden, but while Mary stayed at Mulberry, James went on to Columbia to inform the state legislature of his resignation. Meanwhile, the general assembly had issued a call for elections to select delegates who would consider secession at a December convention. James was quite active helping the state's leaders organize for this election. He himself was elected to represent Camden at that convention.

Mary caught up with her husband in December, at the state's secession convention in Charleston. She had a front row seat on December 20, 1860, when the convention voted unanimously to take South Carolina out of the Union. Once again, James played a key role, helping to draft the state's ordinance of secession. Mary's reaction to these developments was probably typical of many Southerners at that time. She wrote that she felt a "nervous dread & horror of this break with so great a power as U. S. A. but was ready & willing." Mary's comments also indicated that she was something of a reluctant secessionist: "So I was a Seceder—*but* I dreaded the future. . . . My companions had their own thoughts & misgivings doubtless," she mused, "but they breathed fire & defiance." She admitted that South Carolina's secession was almost a necessity, given its past history: "SC had been . . . rampant for years. She was the torment of herself & every body else." Because of such a past, "South Carolina . . . had exasperated & heated themselves [sic] into a fever that only a bloodletting could ever cure." That "fever" swept the state, as Mary soon discovered. Upon her return to Camden, she found that even that backwater was caught up in the excitement. Everywhere, it seemed, men were drilling and marching in preparation for a showdown with the Yankees.

Mary and James did not stay in Camden for long. After the Christmas holidays, James was summoned to Montgomery, Alabama, to participate in the formation of a Southern confederacy. The Provisional Congress, held in February, 1861, also included the representatives of the other six Southern states (Mississippi, Georgia, Alabama, Florida, and Texas) that had seceded in January and early February.

Mary was ecstatic to be surrounded by so much excitement and history-in-the-making. In fact, it was during this time in Montgomery that she decided to keep a journal of the various developments she witnessed, and to record her feelings and reactions to those events. As Mary herself wrote in March, 1861: "[T]his journal is intended to be entirely *objective*. My subjective days are over." She questioned, however, just how wise a decision it was, writing "I think this journal will be disadvantageous for me, for I spend the time now like a spider, spinning my own entrails instead of reading, as my habit was at all spare moments." Still, Mary's dedication to try to be an "objective" chronicler of what she saw would carve her place in history. It resulted in the creation of an unsurpassed first-hand account of the Confederate experience.

Mary was also gratified to be able to witness the increasingly important role James seemed to be taking in the deliberations concerning the new nation. Indeed, James seemed to be the unofficial voice of the South Carolina delegation. Nevertheless, Mary's new enthusiasm for Southern nation-building began to wane after only a few days in the Alabama town because of the way things were evolving. She was troubled by "the kind of men put in office at this crisis." For Mary, the Confederacy's future existence depended upon "Young & active spirits." Instead, she found "When there is an election they hunt up some old fossil ages ago laid on the shelf. There was never such a resurrection of the dead and forgotten." "It is hard for me to believe these people are in earnest," Mary observed ruefully, because so many "sleeping dead head[s]" seemed to be assuming key leadership positions. She remarked candidly on one occasion that she wished "I could put some of my reckless spirit into these discreet, cautious, lazy men." This was not the first nor the last time that Mary would record perceptive—and accurate—descriptions of the Confederacy's leadership.

Mary was also amused and disgusted by the seemingly endless jockeying for position and political preferment. Just after the Provisional Congress met, she wrote that "political manoeuvring [sic] ruled. . . ." "This war began a War of Secession," Mary discovered, but "It will end a War for the Succession of Places." "Everywhere," she concluded, "political intrigue is as rife as in Washington."

THE PEOPLE WHO SO DISAPPOINTED MARY represented most of the white elite in the Deep South at that time; the leadership was comprised, overwhelmingly, of lawyers and planters. Interestingly, the fire-eaters, those who had lobbied so long and hard for secession and the establishment of a Southern nation, were strangely silent or noticeably absent. It was as if they were no longer needed in the Confederate revolution. Now that secession was accomplished, more moderate or conservative men would see to the business of writing a constitution and choosing the new leadership. In many ways, such a development was not all that surprising. The Deep South had always had the reputation for being more radical than the Upper South. Indeed, the secession impulse of early 1861 had been stillborn in states such as Virginia and Tennessee. In order to

convince the people of the Upper South states to join in the
Southern Confederacy, moderation had to rule the day. Consequently, most of the "noodles" Mary detested—the men who took
the reins of leadership—were established, respected men who had
not taken overly radical positions during the late antebellum era and
secession crisis. In fact, James Chesnut was one of those stolid,
respected moderates.

To create a fully functioning government, the first task confronting the men who gathered at Montgomery was to draft a constitution. The Provisional Congress selected a Committee of Twelve,
which included James Chesnut, to perform the task. James played a
key role in these deliberations. Mary reported that James was
"working so hard," and often late into the night, for she "could hear
scratch scratch go the pen" each time she awoke.

Not surprisingly, James and the other members of the committee chose as their model the U.S. Constitution, and adopted most of
its components. They had no quarrel with the Federal Constitution
as originally drafted. They objected only to the way the Northern
majority seemed to be stretching it. Southerners took the road to
secession in order to re-establish the type of small, limited government the Constitution's framers envisioned in 1787. As one scholar
has noted, Southerners regarded the Constitution much as they
viewed the Bible: it was eternal and unchanging, and not liable to
broad interpretation.

Still, the men at Montgomery saw the need for a few changes in
the document. For obvious reasons, slavery was explicitly protected,
although they did prohibit the slave trade. The Confederate framers
also included a provision to allow the president a line-item veto, and
they directed that he serve only one six-year term. This provision
was designed to limit the influence of the chief executive: the
legislature was to remain supreme. Once those basic mechanics had
been ironed out, the representatives turned to the question of who
would fill the top leadership positions of president and vice-president. Again, their selections demonstrated a penchant for moderation. They chose as president Jefferson Davis of Mississippi, a
respected lawyer, planter, Mexican War hero, and one-time U.S.
Senator and secretary of war. Alexander Stephens of Georgia, a

former Whig and friend of Abraham Lincoln, was given the office of vice-president.

By the middle of February 1861, the work of the delegates was complete; it was time to turn to the business of governing under the new order. Once again, Mary's journal reflected the attitudes of most Southerners in the seceded states. She noted, "This southern Confederacy must be supported now by calm determination—& cool brains. We have risked all, & we must play our best for the stake is life or death." Many in the new government hoped that the other Southern states (namely, Virginia, North Carolina, Arkansas, and Tennessee) could be induced eventually to join the Confederacy, but in the late winter of 1861, the prospects did not appear promising. Those states had also held conventions to consider secession, but had voted to wait and see what happened after Lincoln was inaugurated as president.

While they waited, the new Confederate leadership set about establishing the various cabinet offices and departments required of a new nation. Most everyone, including Jefferson Davis, was optimistic about the young nation's future. Davis hoped that the Northern states would allow the seceded states to "go in peace," and many in the North echoed that desire. President-elect Abraham Lincoln, however, did not share those views.

Lincoln was confident, in the days following the formation of the Confederacy, that Unionists throughout the South (and especially in those states which had not seceded by March, 1861), would eventually gain sway, and induce their secession-minded brothers to abandon their drive for independence. He held to that hope until his inauguration on March 4, 1861. In his inaugural address, Lincoln urged reasoned debate and compromise, but he also added that he would protect and defend all federal possessions. It would be on this issue that the two sections would collide.

MARY AND JAMES RETURNED TO MULBERRY shortly after Lincoln was inaugurated, but they did not stay there long. Trading his politician's broadcloth for the butternut uniform of the Confederate Army, James accepted an appointment to General Pierre G. T. Beauregard's staff, and was ordered to report to Charleston, flashpoint of the sectional crisis. Mary followed him to the "City By the Sea," and thus was once again center stage at a dramatic moment in history.

The situation in Charleston had been tense for several months. A federal garrison at Fort Moultrie had refused to surrender to South Carolina authorities after the state's secession, and on December 27, 1860, had relocated secretly from Fort Moultrie to a fort deemed more defensible, Fort Sumter, which was located on an island in the harbor. The fort and its status in Charleston Harbor remained a hot topic of debate in both South Carolina and Washington. By early April 1861, supplies in the fort were running low, which prompted the federal commander, Major Robert Anderson, to request re-provisioning. President Lincoln notified Governor Francis Pickens of South Carolina that he was sending supplies to Fort Sumter, but he promised the governor that he would not send any more troops. Governor Pickens relayed this information to President Davis, who ordered Beauregard to demand the evacuation of the fort. James Chesnut was one of the officers Beauregard chose to row out to Sumter to deliver this ultimatum. Anderson refused to leave the fort. The following morning, on April 12, at 4:30 a.m., Beauregard ordered the shore batteries at Charleston to open fire. The war had begun.

Mary, who was staying at the Mills House Hotel, spent several sleepless nights in Charleston before the bombardment commenced. She knew James was involved in the negotiations and she worried about the outcome. As she tossed and turned in the early morning hours of April 12, she heard the church bells from St. Michael's toll, and realized the deadline for a resolution to the crisis was approaching: "If Anderson does not accept terms—at four—the orders are—he shall be fired upon." She went on to record, "I count four—St. Michael chimes. I begin to hope. At half-past four, the heaving booming of cannon." When Mary heard the cannon fire, "I sprang out of bed. And on my knees—prostrate—I prayed as I never prayed before." Mary would not stay in that position for long. Her prayers were soon interrupted by the "sound of stir all over the house—pattering of feet in the corridor—all seemed hurrying one way. I put on my double gown and a shawl and went, too." Mary hurried to the

James Chesnut, Jr., in the uniform of a Confederate brigadier general. Courtesy of the South Caroliniana Library, University of South Carolina.

roof of the hotel to watch the drama unfold. "The shells were bursting" over Charleston Harbor and the fort. The scene was bedlam: "The women were wild, there on the housetop. Prayers from the women and imprecations from the men, and then a shell would light up the scene. Tonight, they say, the forces are to attempt to land." What worried Mary most, however, was that James was "rowing about in a boat somewhere in that dark bay." She could not be certain whether he was in danger from the Southern batteries or not. Fort Sumter, Mary noted, "did not fire a shot."

Slowly, dawn approached, and still the bombardment continued. Not until 1:30 p.m. on the afternoon of April 13, when Fort Sumter was filled with flames, did Major Anderson raise a flag of surrender. The next day Anderson's garrison and the exultant South Carolina troops watched as the United States flag was lowered and the Federal garrison was taken prisoner. Miraculously, no one was injured during the bombardment. The reaction in Charleston was immediate—and jubilant. All rejoiced that the South had proved victorious in this first confrontation, and with no loss of life. As Mary recorded on April 15, "I did not know that one could live [through] such days of excitement."

While Charleston rejoiced, the Lincoln administration acted. The day after Fort Sumter surrendered, Lincoln issued a call for 75,000 ninety-day volunteers to "suppress" the rebellion. Almost immediately thereafter, Virginia, Tennessee, North Carolina, and Arkansas called special conventions to consider secession. Lincoln's call, it seemed, was the overt sign of Northern aggression for which they were waiting. By the beginning of May, the Confederacy had gained four new states. Representatives of those states joined the others who convened in Montgomery at the spring session of the Provisional Congress of the Confederate States of America. Mary and James also attended this gathering because James represented South Carolina in the Congress. It was during this meeting that the states voted to relocate the capital from sleepy Montgomery to the larger, more cosmopolitan city of Richmond. Interestingly, three states voted against this proposal, including South Carolina. Mary noted that James "oppose[d] it violently because this [Montgomery] is so central a position for our government." Mary, however, saw other, more valid reasons for the change in location: "I see these uncomfortable hotels will move the Congress. Our statesmen love their ease. And it will be so hot here in the summer." Neither she—nor anyone else apparently—foresaw that the move would dictate the strategy of the entire war.

Mary and James spent three weeks in Montgomery, and then returned to Camden and Mulberry. Initially, Mary was delighted with the change of scene. She found Montgomery, and their rooms in the hotel, an "abode of misery." She tactfully told the local residents of the town how much she loved it, but privately, she thought otherwise. The Alabama town was too small, too dirty, and too provincial after the cultivated atmosphere of Charleston or Washington. At home in South Carolina she could have breakfast in her room, with "pure white house linen, cream in coffee, & good coffee, *luxuries* when one comes out of a *den* of abominations such as we have lived in Montgomery Hall." Mary's delight at returning to the pleasures of servants and refined living would soon pale, however. Shortly after going home to Mulberry she noted in her journal that "One day here is so like another I forget I have a journal—& at Montgomery & Charleston *events, witticisms,* &c are so rapidly following each other's heels I have no time to record them." For Mary, plantation life at Mulberry was unduly sedate and entirely uneventful, especially during such exciting times.

Mary would stay in Camden only until the end of June. By that time, James had already gone to the new capital in Richmond to seek another assignment. Unwilling to remain alone in South Carolina when she could join James in the new seat of power, Mary wrote to a friend and instructed her to find the Chesnuts suitable accomodations in Richmond. By the end of June, Mary was back at the young Confederacy's center stage.

The city to which Mary journeyed was an old one. Nestled at the falls of the James River, Richmond had long been noted as a tobacco entrepôt. But by 1860, railroads and the iron and grain milling industries had also made Richmond an industrial and commercial center. With almost 38,000 inhabitants, Richmond ranked among the South's urban leaders in terms of population, wealth, and stature. It was also a political city. Thomas Jefferson had designed the state capitol, and thus it bore the imprimatur of the author of the Declaration of Independence. Still, the city maintained the aura and influence of the planter elite. Many locals remarked that for all of Richmond's modernity, it was still a haven for the Southern white upper class, the First Families of Virginia.

As the new Confederate capital, Richmond was alive with activity. People from all over the South flocked there to seek employment in the new war bureaucracies, or a more elevated post within the government. Mary was especially pleased to be in the new capital because it meant a reunion with old and dear friends from James's U.S. Senate days, and with the new acquaintances the Chesnuts had made in Montgomery. Almost immediately, Mary was thrust into a round of visiting and parties, and she loved every minute of it.

One of her first outings set the tone for her sojourn in the capital city. She accompanied Mrs. Martha Stanard, considered by many to be the most wealthy and prominent hostess in the city, on an afternoon ride out to a Confederate troop encampment. The carriage ride was significant for Mary's observations:

> A man riding a beautiful horse joined us. He wore a hat with somehow a military look to it. He sat his horse gracefully, and he was so distinguished . . . that I very much regretted not catching his name as Mrs. Stanard gave it to us. He, however, heard ours and bowed as gracefully as he rode, and the few remarks he made to each of us showed he knew all about us.
>
> But Mrs. Stanard was in ecstasies of pleasureable excitement. I felt she had bagged a big fish. Just then they abounded in Richmond.

After the gentleman bid farewell, Mary immediately inquired of her companion who the handsome officer was. " 'You do not know!', Mrs. Stanard replied more than a bit incredulously. 'Why it is Robert E. Lee. . . .' " Mary's later recorded comments indicate she was not, initially at least, as captivated as her friend: "All the same, I like Smith Lee [Robert E. Lee's brother] better, and I like his looks, too. I know Smith Lee well," she wrote. "Can anybody say they know his brother? I doubt it. He looks so cold and quiet and grand."

Such encounters with the leading luminaries of the capital would continue to delight Mary. Richmond, with all its fascinating and prominent people, had the excitement and diversions that Camden, and especially Mulberry, lacked. As Mary herself noted, "I am enjoying the noise & bustle of a city" again.

While Mary enjoyed getting reacquainted with people such as Jefferson and Varina Davis, James was busy with military affairs on Beauregard's staff. By the beginning of July, it was increasingly evident that the South's fond hopes for a bloodless struggle for independence were illusory. A large force of Federal troops had moved across the Potomac and was attempting to trap Confederate forces under Beauregard before he could be reinforced by General Joseph E. Johnston, who was in the Shenandoah Valley. While the rival armies jockeyed for position, James grew concerned. In letters to Mary, he spoke repeatedly about the weaknesses of the green Confederate Army. Mary reflected his concern. She recorded that the Union Army "grew stronger every day." At the same time, the Confederates seemed "to grow *weaker.*" The cause, as Mary knew, was not hard to find. The Southern armies lacked equipment— guns, cannon, and ammunition. These early problems in manufacturing and supply would be eased as the war progressed and as Southern factories began to increase production of war materiel. But Mary had hit upon a key problem that would not go away: the failure of the Confederacy to produce enough of the implements of war to sustain its armies.

Despite her—and James's—worries about the unpreparedness of the Southern army, the Confederates proved victorious in their first real engagement with Federal troops. Johnston managed to slip through the Federal trap set for him in the Shenandoah Valley, and joined Beauregard on the field at Manassas Junction on the banks of Bull Run creek. The battle that ensued on July 21 was really little more than a clash between two armed mobs. Both the Union troops and the Confederate soldiers were young and inexperienced. They had spent little time before the engagement learning the rudiments of drill or basic maneuvers when under fire. Moreover, many were unused to the heat and humidity that July in Virginia could bring. Straggling was a major problem for both armies, as was a failure to get the troops into position where they were needed. And Beauregard's rather convuluted battle plan did not help. Despite such problems, the Confederates emerged victorious, in no small part because of the heroic stand of Colonel Thomas J. Jackson's troops on Henry House Hill. Jackson became a legend that day, and was forever after known as "Stonewall."

Mary learned of the Battle of Manassas in her Richmond hotel room. She had been ill for several days, but had managed to keep abreast of the developments in northern Virginia through friends who visited her. Varina Davis told her of the "great battle" fought less than thirty miles outside of Washington. The news, Mary recalled, "got me up." "Times were too wild with excitement," she wrote, "to stay in bed."

Two days later, James returned from the battlefield to give Mary an eye-witness account of the South's great victory. That same day, she joined her husband at what Mary considered a "brilliant" reception at the White House of the Confederacy. The Davises hosted the party as a celebration in honor of the Confederacy's first major battlefield success. Mary recorded that the president addressed a large group of well-wishers about the triumph. She noted wryly that "the President took all the credit to himself for the victory," a stand that would later prove quite unpopular with some of his generals. She went on to relate that Davis told the attentive group that the "wounded roused & shouted for Jeff Davis—& the men rallied at the sight of him & rushed on & routed the enemy." Mary added, with a hint of amusement, that "Jeff Davis was . . . two miles from the battlefield" during the contest. As Mary well knew, the president was "greedy for military fame." In fact, he had hoped to be the commander of a major Confederate army, instead of the civilian commander-in-chief of all Confederate forces.

For Mary, the highlight of the evening was the attention showered on James. She wrote "I felt so proud of my husband last night— & so happy." James had been summoned by the throng of celebrants "& gave a capital speech. He gave the glory of the victory to Beauregard—& said if the President had not said so much for him self he would have praised him."

Rejoicing was the order of the day throughout Richmond. For almost everyone, the Confederate victory was proof of the superiority of the Southern army and the Southern cause. It seemed to reinforce the rather prevalent belief that one Southerner could whip seven Yankees. In Washington, the reaction to the defeat was one of disbelief. Most were stunned that the Federals had been routed so ingloriously, and many feared that the Confederates would follow up their victory with a march on Washington. For Lincoln and his War Department, Manassas revealed the need for army reorganization. The Union had to prepare for a long, drawn out conflict.

While the North buckled up for a fight, the Confederates wallowed in pride and overconfidence. Too many came to believe that the Yankees were weak cowards who could not stand up to the dedicated, independence-minded Confederates. Overconfidence would seriously hurt the Confederate cause in the short term.

Not all Confederates were sanguine that the war would be a short and victorious one. Jefferson Davis was one of the few in Richmond who believed, as did his Northern counterpart, that the conflict would be a protracted affair, and he confessed as much to Mary during an evening reception he and Varina hosted. At that gathering, Mary observed that Davis spoke of the "pluck and muscle, endurance, and dogged courage—dash and red-hot patriotism" of Southern troops. Still, Mary detected a "sad refrain" throughout the course of his remarks. That melancholy, she concluded, was a result of Davis's conviction that many battles would be fought and many Southern lives lost before independence would be achieved. Mary reflected the thinking of most Southerners in the summer of 1861: "That floored me at once. [The war] has been too long for me already," she admitted, despite the fact that only about six months had passed since the formal creation of the Confederacy. What also troubled Mary was Davis's belief that "before the end came, we would have many a bitter experience. He said only fools doubted the courage of the Yankees or their willingness to fight when they saw fit." Davis felt sure that since the South had "roused them [the Northerners] . . . they will fight like the devils."

Mary may have been disturbed by Davis's remarks, but she had other concerns as well. Like so many other women in the Confederate capital and elsewhere in the South, Mary was active in hospital work. She stayed in close contact with Mrs. George Randolph, president of the Richmond Ladies Association. That organization collected donations of food, bandages, and other goods, and distributed them to the Confederate wounded in local hospitals. Mary participated in those activities and also made the rounds at the hospitals, dispensing food and good cheer to the recuperating soldiers. She noted a typical visit in her journal in late August of 1861: "To day have been all day at the Hospitals. Such a day. . . . saw sick men with measles, typhus fever & dinner tables & all horrors all in one room—dreadful. . . ." On that day as on others, Mary took a particular interest in the wounded from South Carolina, and made it a point to attend to their needs above others. Though she tried to maintain an air of cheerfulness during all her visits, the plight of the men, and the horrible conditions of the hospitals she frequented, had an impact on her. "I can never again shut out of view the sights I saw of human misery, " Mary wrote. "I sit thinking, shut my eyes, and see it all. . . . long rows of ill men on cots. Ill of . . . every human ailment. . . . long rows [too] of them dead, dying. Awful smells, awful sights." Despite such horrors that would only grow worse as the war continued, Mary visited the hospitals as often as she could. She also participated in the "knitting *mania*" that seemed to infect every Southern woman. "You never see a woman," Mary noted, "without her needles going." Every one, from the wealthiest society matron to the humblest yeoman's wife participated in the knitting "bees."

As important as the work Mary and other Southern women accomplished, it still seemed to pale in comparison to the great contributions Southern men were making to the Confederate cause. Mary recorded in her journal, "I think *these* times make women feel their humiliation in the affairs of the world. With *men* it is on to the field—'glory, honour, praise, &c, power.' Women can only stay home. . . . How are the daughters of Eve punished." On another occasion, Mary wrote patriotically that if she were a man, she would have sought a battlefield commission—and a hero's role: "I should have either been killed at once or made a name & done some good for my country. Lord Nelson's motto would have been mine," Mary concluded. "Victory—or Westminster Abbey."

For someone as intelligent and ambitious as Mary Chesnut, the subordinate role she had to assume in Southern society was a bitter pill to swallow. Nonetheless, the war years did mark a watershed of sorts in women's roles and activities. As the war continued, more and more women were called upon to assume greater responsibilities. With the men "on to the field," there was often no choice but to tap women for jobs once reserved for men. They began their new duties, as Mary, in hospitals as assistants or as nurses. Soon, however, they would be serving in government offices as clerks, or in factories sewing uniforms or manufacturing war materiel, such as gun cartridges. Women left behind in the countryside took charge of the family farm or the plantation, and frequently had to direct the overseer and the slaves as to what needed to be done. Though these women initially sought advice from their husbands and fathers, as time passed, they became more confident of their own abilities to make decisions and manage affairs.

Class and social status seemed to matter little, as women of all social ranks joined the effort to help the Southern cause. Still, there were class differences in the types of jobs women assumed, and in their perceptions of the work they and others did. For the wealthier segment, the work women did—in hospitals, for example—was more in keeping with the traditions of plantation paternalism and women's benevolent organizations. Many well-to-do women also sought work in the various Confederate government bureaus. Although those posts were supposed to be filled by women who had a genuine financial need, more often than not they were given to women from well-connected families who had political or military influence. Interestingly, not all upper class women regarded such government positions as plum assignments. Mary Chesnut and one of her wealthy Columbia friends were determined, "come what will, survive or perish—we will not go into one of the departments. We will not stand up all day at a table and cut notes apart, ordered round by a department clerk. . . . [We will do] Any menial service—under the shadow of our own rooftree. Department—never!"

For other women, working on the farm or in the factory was often a matter of economic survival; changes in traditional gender roles were a necessity in order to sustain and support their families.

Regardless of the reason, throughout the war women assumed a wider variety of roles, some out of a sense of duty, and some out of a need to survive. In the process, they moved farther away from their antebellum stereotype of languid "Southern belles." Still, one wonders if these women honestly believed or hoped that their extraordinary efforts would continue after peace returned. More likely, there was probably some type of unspoken consensus among them—as well as the men—that changes in roles were a necessary response to an emergency situation. The post-war return to the status quo antebellum in gender spheres indicates that all the changes women precipitated during the war were of a rather transitory nature.

MARY'S CONTINUED FRUSTRATION WITH HER subordinate role in military matters was exacerbated by James's lack of interest in his own military career. Much to Mary's chagrin, James became bored with his military assignment in the late summer of 1861, and he seemed unwilling to lobby President Davis for a new post. James's indecision bothered Mary tremendously. She had hoped that he would take a more active role on his own behalf in order to garner a diplomatic post to either Britain or France. Mary even contemplated the possibility that he would be appointed to a cabinet position. But her ambitions for her husband were not to be fulfilled. South Carolina political leaders convinced James that he could best serve his nation by being elected to the Confederate Senate. In response to their entreaties, he returned to South Carolina and embarked upon a rather half-hearted effort to be elected to the 1862 session of the Confederate Congress.

Mary greeted these developments with mixed emotions. Longing to revisit London and Paris, she had secretly hoped that he would get a diplomatic assignment (She confided to her journal in mid-August, "I wish Mr. Davis would send *me* to Paris"). She was thus quite disappointed when those positions went to James M. Mason and John Slidell. She worried that the political feuds within South Carolina, and the opposition of certain state leaders to the Davis administration, would also affect James detrimentally. Mary alternated between bemoaning the possibility of being exiled to

South Carolina with its "stillness & torpor," and trying to put the best face on her feelings. "I am trying to look *defeat* of my personal ambition in the face," she admitted, "[s]o if it does come I can better bear it! & if it does not come the rebound will be so much more delightful." Still, Mary recognized her feelings for what they were: a symptom of her aspirations for James—and herself—to have more power and privilege. With true insight, she asked herself, "Why was I born so frightfully ambitious[?]"

Mary's worst fears were realized in early December, 1861, when James was defeated in his bid for the Senate. Mary was devastated. On the day the results became known, she jotted down her innermost thoughts. "I am up again after my heavy fall. No bones broken, no dislocation—but sore & stunned yet—*inward* bruises." What bothered her most—besides the fact that she would have to return to Mulberry and "provincial sloth"—was the reality that "This is an end of JC's political life." Mary did not know how he could serve the Confederacy within the inner circles of power while mired in the backwaters of South Carolina. She continued to dwell on this defeat, and eventually, came to blame herself. She was certain that her excessive ambition and arrogance had caused this reversal in James's political fortunes, and admitted to her journal, "I had grown insufferable with my arrogance." As she reread some old letters, Mary noted how she had changed over the course of her married life. She recorded her self-evaluation in her journal: "What a meek, humble little thing I was—how badly JC played his cards to let me develop into the self-sufficient thing I am now. For I think this bitter drop [the defeat] was for *me*. He will care very little. . . ."

While Mary reflected on what James's defeat would mean for her—and his future public career—1861 drew to a close. To be sure, it had been an eventful year, and she had witnessed first hand many of the momentous developments of those twelve months. But for Mary, the year ended on a very depressing note, with the reality of being relegated to the provincialism of Camden and Mulberry. "I can already feel the awful effect of that stillness & *torpor* piercing to the marrow of my bones," she confessed candidly to her journal. Not until well into the new year of 1862 would that "torpor" abate.

Chapter Four

---O---

1862:
"We Have No Breathing
Time Given Us"

DESPITE JAMES'S LOSS IN THE SENATE RACE, he was still considered one of South Carolina's leading political figures. Because of that status, the South Carolina secession convention appointed James to the executive council and made him chief of the state's military department on January 9, 1862. The council was, in theory, a five man body that was to oversee the state's defensive preparations and war mobilization. In reality, it represented the convention's attempt to hamstring Governor Francis Pickens in his exercise of leadership. Mary seemed more aware of problems inherent in this arrangement than James. In all of her correspondence and journal entries, she referred to the executive council rather derisively as the "guard of honor." What bothered Mary most was the possibility that James's acceptance of the post would place him on the political "shelf," perhaps "forever!" Such fears were not entirely groundless, for the opposition to the council seemed to grow with every passing day. Still, James did what he believed to be his duty, and accepted the position. Shortly after his acceptance, he journeyed to Columbia to take up his new assignment. Mary went on to Mulberry, and promptly fell ill. She attributed it to "dullness striking in."

Mary did not remain at Mulberry long. Soon, she was back in Columbia with James, and the excitement of the state capital made her ill health a thing of the past. For Mary, "This Columbia is the place for good living—pleasant people, pleasant dinners, pleasant drives. . . . This is the most hospitable place in the world." While James worked on such matters as procuring laborers to build fortifications and obtaining goods for South Carolina troops, Mary busied herself with hospital work. She also continued to sew clothing for the soldiers. But even as she aided those left behind, Mary kept an eye on developments elsewhere in the Confederacy, and what she saw was disturbing.

CONFEDERATE AFFAIRS HAD SEEMED BRIGHT in the aftermath of Manassas, but by fall 1861, things darkened as Port Royal on the South Carolina coast fell to Federal forces. The situation did not improve in the new year. Instead, Confederate fortunes seemed to take a steady downward turn. In February, 1862, Southerners received word that Roanoke Island had also fallen into enemy hands. Then, everyone watched as a combined river and land movement began against Fort Henry on the Tennessee River and Fort Donelson on the Cumberland River. Confederate armies in the west seemed to be falling back, away from Kentucky and toward the Confederate heartland in Tennessee. These reverses caused Mary to record in early February that, "Confederate affairs [are] in a blue way." She noted, too, that the Mississippi River, the South's lifeline, was also threatened by the Federal navy: "New armies, [and] new fleets, [are] swarming and threatening everywhere." Mary could only react to such developments with dismay, and a renewed determination to avoid the worst: "[we must] be willing to do as much to save ourselves from a nauseous union with them as they are willing to do by way of revengeful coercion in forcing us back." Still, Mary admitted that "Bad news is killing me."

The bad news continued to the end of February and into the spring. Federal gunboats under Flag Officer Andrew Foote succeeded in taking lightly defended Fort Henry on February 6, 1862. Fort Donelson was better built and fortified than Henry, but it, too, fell to the Union's new hero, General Ulysses S. Grant, on February 16. With Fort Donelson gone, the river approaches to Nashville were left wide open. After the fall of the two forts, the theater's Confederate commander, General Albert Sidney Johnston, believed that his options for defending middle Tennessee were gone. He withdrew his army all the way to northern Mississippi. Johnston's withdrawal led to the evacuation and abandonment of the Tennessee state capital at Nashville, almost without firing a shot. It was a serious loss, for Nashville contained many important factories and quartermaster depots that were essential to the mobilization effort. As Mary noted on February 25, "Given up: Nashville. . . . And they have taken at Nashville more men than we had at Manassas.* Bad handling of troops—we poor women think, or it could not be." More ominously, Mary thought, the Confederacy "cannot replace" the troops that were lost. Southerners were stunned by the news, but worse was yet to come.

Johnston, at his base near Corinth, Mississippi, made plans for an offensive that would allow the Confederates to reclaim Tennessee. He hoped to surprise Grant with a massive assault on Grant's forces at Pittsburg Landing (located on the Tennessee River), near Shiloh, Tennessee. Johnston did, in fact, catch Grant unaware on April 6, and succeeded in driving the Federal forces all the way back to the river bank. But after that initial success, the attack stalled, aided undoubtedly by Johnston's mortal wounding. James Chesnut's old commander, P. G. T. Beauregard, succeeded Johnston to command. Beauregard, however, was unable to withstand Grant's April 7 counterattack against the Confederate positions. With Grant receiving reinforcements and Confederate casualties running high, Beauregard believed he had no choice but to withdraw the Confederate Army back to its base in northern Mississippi.

News of Shiloh shocked people on either side of the Mason–Dixon line. Both armies suffered such heavy casualties that the battle made all other engagements up to April of 1862 seem bloodless by comparison: Federal losses reached 13,000, while Confederate casualties exceeded 10,700 over the course of the two-day battle.

*This claim was based on an unfounded rumor exaggerating the losses.

For the Union and the Confederacy, Shiloh represented a significant turning point. It was obvious to Northerners and Southerners alike that this would not be a short war. Now most acknowledged that the conflict was destined to be long and bloody. Perhaps because of that realization, Shiloh also triggered a new approach to the war. Each side strove to mold amateur, green recruits into skilled and disciplined veterans. This change marked a dramatic departure from 1861, when untrained mobs met on the fields of First Manassas.

Southerners had just digested the results of Shiloh when they were rocked by more bad news: Fort Pulaski, guarding the approaches to Savannah, fell to Federal control on April 11. Worse tidings came less than two weeks later, when Southerners were stunned to learn that on April 25, New Orleans, the Confederacy's largest city and busiest port, had succumbed to David Farragut and the West Gulf Blockading Squadron (largely as a result of these successes, Farragut would be promoted the Navy's first admiral on July 16, 1862). Everywhere, it appeared, the Confederacy was under attack—and losing key strategic points to the Union onslaught.

As Mary watched these developments, she alternated between despair, outrage, and disgust. "Every morning's paper enough to kill a well woman [or] age a strong and hearty one," she wrote after learning about the events in Tennessee. "Battle after battle—disaster after disaster" seemed to be the reality throughout much of the spring. Mary noted that some blamed poor military leadership for the string of Confederate reverses. She, however, believed that the fault lay elsewhere. After learning of the fall of New Orleans, she observed:

> The Confederacy [is being] done to death by the politicians. What wonder we are lost. Those wretched creatures the Congress and the legislature could never rise to the greatness of the occasion. They seem to think they were in a neighborhood squabble about precedence.

What infuriated Mary most was her belief that the politicians were only "busy as bees about their own places or their personal honor—too busy to see the enemy at a distance." Moreover, they were guilty of "forgetting the interest of the people they represent." She even went so far as to doubt the efficacy of representative government during wartime—especially the Confederacy's—stating bitterly at one point: "Republics—everybody jawing, everybody putting their mouths in, nothing sacred, all confusion of babble, crimination, and recrimination—republics can't carry on war."

In a sense, Mary had gotten to the crux of the problem: the unraveling of support for the Confederacy among both politicians and plain folk as Southern military success turned into misfortune. Southerners had always been a diverse group, but Lincoln's election and the perceived threat to Southern liberty and Southern interests had forged unity among all Southerners. Indeed, the South was perhaps never so unified behind a cause than it was behind the Confederacy after Fort Sumter. But that unity was a fragile one, created largely out of opposition to a common enemy, the North. Different perceptions of what the Confederacy meant, what it should constitute, and how it should operate were overshadowed by the outburst of Southern patriotism that followed victories at Fort Sumter and First Manassas.

Perhaps predictably, the outpouring of nationalism and support for the Confederate cause were tempered by defeat. That was the reality by early 1862. The decline of military fortunes prompted many within the Confederate government to seek the reason for the South's reversals. Since the Confederate cause was just, so the logic went, there had to be some palpable explanation for the South's defeats. Some in the Congress decided President Jefferson Davis was the culprit. They took the offensive, and criticized Davis strongly for his governmental policies; they also questioned his overall military strategy.

According to recent scholarship on the Confederate government, the debates that flared during 1862 were significant for what they symbolized: a far-reaching discussion over the meaning of the Confederate experiment. Many who criticized the president for real and imagined infringements of personal liberty and state sovereignty feared that war would create a large, centralized tyranny. Others, including most notably, Jefferson Davis, believed that wartime required an expansion of governmental power. The result was a noxious political atmosphere that saw the president get most of his policies enacted, but at a high cost: increased factiousness that affected virtually every level of government, and which, over time, disgusted and disillusioned the common folk. This situation would continue and grow worse as Confederate losses mounted.

For his part, Davis's actions did little to end the relentless criticism he was subjected to by the Congress, the press, and ultimately, the Southern people. Perhaps more than any other Southerner, Davis saw the need for concentrated power to direct the war effort. He eventually created a government as highly centralized as that which Lincoln directed. But too often, Davis was unable to communicate effectively the need for his actions to either the Congress or the people. In fact, he frequently could not convince his friends in Congress to rally to his defense.

Mary had perceived the tension between some members of the Congress and Davis even before the Southern battlefield defeats of 1862. In Montgomery, she had recorded that it was "a pity—these men [Confederate politicians] have brought old hatreds & grudges & spites from the old Union. Already we see they will willingly injure our cause to hurt Jeff Davis." Things changed very little after the capital was moved to Richmond. Mary noted that the strain between Davis and prominent, powerful politicians such as Louis T. Wigfall of Texas was beginning to show. Often the criticism of the president went beyond the political and became personal in nature. Many started to snipe at both Davis and his wife, Varina, for their seeming lack of social graces.

The number of the Davises' critics, not to mention the nature of the criticisms, grew more hostile and strident as the war progressed and as Southern defeats increased. Though Mary had once been counted among those critical of the Davises (she had cattily remarked at one point that the Davises were "coarse talking people," who "prov[ed] themselves any thing but well bred by their talk."), she quickly became one of their warmest friends and staunchest advocates. Indeed, the president, perhaps aware that she was more supportive than others around him, would seek out Mary for long chats, and Varina would count on Mary's friendship as dark clouds swirled around the Southern nation. Predictably, as she grew closer to the first couple, she became more outspoken against their detractors. While in Columbia, Mary would castigate all that city's malcontents, stating bitterly, "I do not know a half-dozen men who would not gaily step into Jeff Davis's shoes, with a firm conviction they could do better in every respect than he does. The monstrous conceit, the fatuous ignorance of these critics!" Mary's unwavering defense of Davis continued from 1862 until her death two and a half decades later.

THE CONFEDERACY'S DIMMING PROSPECTS did not prevent Southerners, including Mary, from discussing the causes of secession and war. Mary believed that Northerners mistook the motivation and ideology behind Southern secession. She reported that a high ranking Union general had stated bluntly that the war was " 'an attempt to extend the area of slavery.' " Mary rejected that notion. "Can that be," she asked, none too rhetorically, "when not one-third of our volunteer army are slave-owners—and not one-third of that third who does not dislike slavery as much as Mrs. Stowe . . . ?"* Her assessment of the composition of Confederate ranks was not off the mark. The vast majority of the Confederate Army was composed of men who had little if any tangible connection to slavery and the planter elite. For these white yeomen, the real issues were defense of their homes and a protection of their "way of life"—however they might define it. To be sure, many undoubtedly aspired to slaveholder status. That was, after all, a sign of upward mobility and social prestige in the nineteenth-century South. But more important, middle class farmers, not to mention other Southerners, feared the consequences that emancipation would bring. They were firmly convinced that only race war or economic competition for limited land and resources could result from the manumission of the slaves. Those fears impelled the independent white middle class to take up arms and die for the Confederate cause.

For Mary, as for most Southerners, the true purpose of fighting was "to shake off the yoke of foreign invaders." For that reason alone, she noted, "we consider our cause righteous." Mary went on to observe that "The Yankees since the war has begun have discovered it is to free the slaves." She realized that this new war aim allowed

*Chesnut refers here to Harriet Beecher Stowe, author of *Uncle Tom's Cabin*.

Northerners to consider "their cause . . . noble." But, she added rather tellingly, "[The Yankees] also expect to make the war pay." She felt that, "Yankees" were rarely motivated by any crusade that "does not pay." Again echoing many of her countrymen, she believed that the Southern people had for years been victims of greedy Northern political and financial interests: "They think we belong to them," she wrote. "We have been good milk cows" [over the years]. Milked," she contended in a tone reminiscent of her father, the nullifier, "by the tariff. . . . We let them have all the hard earnings. We bore the ban of slavery. They got the money. . . . secondhand they received the wages of slavery. [While] [t]hey grew rich," Mary concluded, "we grew poor."

Although she stoutly defended the cause of the South, the war did not change Mary's attitude toward slavery. She hated slavery because of its moral implications. It created a sexual double standard in the South that encouraged miscegenation. When Mary wrote, "we live surrounded by prostitutes," she referred to the slave women who were so often the prey of white slaveholders. She went on to note:

> Like the patriarchs of old our men live all in one house with their wives and their concubines, and the mulattoes one sees in every family exactly resemble the white children—and every lady tells you who is the father of all the mulatto children in everybody's household.

She was critical of the women who ignored the crossbreeding within their own households. A Southern lady often could not admit to herself, let alone others, that her "upstanding" husband was in reality assaulting slave women: "[T]hose [mulatto children] in her own [home] she seems to think drop from the clouds. . . ."

Mary kept a close eye on the slaves in her household as the war progressed to see if they were aware of events as they unfolded. She found that "Not by one word or look can we detect any change in the[ir] demeanor." Still, she wondered if their indifference or disinterest was genuine: "Are they stolidly stupid," Mary asked, "or wiser than we are, silent and strong biding their time?" On another occasion, Mary observed that the slaves at Mulberry had faces "as unreadable as the sphinx . . . they are placid, docile, kind, and obedient."

Mary came to question her trust in the Chesnut servants after she received word that slaves had murdered her cousin Betsy Witherspoon in her sleep. Yet, her comments in the aftermath of Witherspoon's death are instructive, for they demonstrated a subtle brand of paternalism and racism, not to mention naivete, that was common among most members of the planter elite: "Hitherto I have never thought of being afraid of negroes. I had never injured any of them. Why should they want to hurt me?" Mary went on to note with a touch of sanctimony that "Two-thirds of my religion consists in trying to be good to negroes because they are so in my power." Still, she realized, perhaps as a result of the murder, that slaves were not the passive, child-like lumps of flesh she thought and expected them to be. That awareness shattered her previous sense of safety and well-being. She wrote that "Somehow . . . I feel that the ground is cut away from under my feet. Why should they treat me any better than they have done Cousin Betsy . . . ?" Later, Mary conceded that with the servants, "We take our chance, doing our duty as best we may. . . ."

Mary made no attempt to hide her feelings about slavery in public, a stance that was often unpopular with many of her friends and her husband's political associates. At the same time, she was quite critical of Northern abolitionists who continued to heap abuse upon the South and Southerners. On numerous occasions, she used her journals to counter the allegations of people such as Harriet Beecher Stowe, Ralph Waldo Emerson, and Horace Greeley. One such entry accused those individuals of being closed up "in nice New England homes. . . . shut up in libraries, writing books which ease their hearts of their bitterness to us." She would remark rather acidly, "What self denial do they practice?" She concluded that what those writers accomplished was "the cheapest philanthropy trade in the world. . . . Easy as setting John Brown to come down here and cut our throats in Christ's name." Mary went on to describe what she believed to be the reality on Southern plantations, based upon her observations of her own family:

These people were educated at Northern schools mostly—read the same Northern books as their Northern contemners [sic], the same daily newspapers, the same Bible—have the same ideas of right and wrong—are highbred, lovely, good, pious— doing their duty as they conceive it. They live in negro villages. They do not preach and teach hate as gospel and the sacred duty of murder and insurrection, but they strive to ameliorate the condition of these Africans in every particular. They set the example of a perfect life—life of utter self-abnegation. . . . They have a swarm of blacks about them as children under their care—not as Mrs. Stowe's fancy paints them, but the hard, unromantic, undeveloped, savage Africans. And they hate slavery worse than Mrs. Stowe.

Mary concluded that "I say we are no better than our judges North—*and no worse.*"

To be sure, Mary's comments and criticisms contain the type of defensive and prejudicial language one would expect from a nineteenth-century Southerner. But it is the reality of her life as a Southern woman, as much as the content of her remarks, that is most significant. Even as she condemned both slavery and abolitionists with an even-handed sense of justice, she was nevertheless utterly dependent upon the institution she claimed to abhor. Mary would discuss in her journals the chores she assigned her maids Molly and Ellen, or James's servant Laurence; she would note that "Your own servants think for you, they know your ways and your wants; they save you all responsibility, even in matters of your own ease and well-doing"; she would make it a point to record when she had actually done something for herself, because it was so extraordinary, and because it demonstrated to her "how dreadful it would be without her [Ellen] *if I should have to do it all.*" In this way, her attitudes and actions were little altered from her younger years. Mary might rail against slavery and its harmful effects on Southern society and morals, and she might refer to slaves and slave character in blatantly racist and derogatory terms, but she was still dependent upon both the slave and the institution. Indeed, her status as a Southern gentlewoman and member of the elite was directly linked to her husband's ownership of slaves. Although she may have understood this inconsistency, she was never able to resolve it.

Slavery was not the only issue that frequented Mary's thoughts. She had always been a keen student of history, and during the war, she became quite interested in military affairs. Her voracious reading allowed her to develop a good grasp of the military strategy she read about in the newspapers. Quite frequently, she would record her musings in her journals. Her comments demonstrate a careful reading of the situation and a highly developed intellect that embraced a wealth of subjects. Mary believed that the South had great advantages in geography because of the abundant "swamps, forests, [and] rivers." As she correctly discerned, these natural barriers could be used to the South's benefit to thwart an invading army. She would soon learn, however, that those same barriers that discouraged invasion in the Virginia theater acted as natural invasion corridors in the West.

Mary's interest in the past also caused her to reflect upon the historical precedents of great national struggles. She found encouragement in the fact that "persistent, united people," such as the Athenians at Marathon, had succeeded in defeating larger and better equipped enemy forces. But for every instance of success, there was also an example of failure. As Mary discovered, "[there was] the Roman muster roll in the Punic Wars. Seven hundred thousand foot, seventy thousand horse [soldiers]." She feared that in that analogy, the North, with its resources of men and materiel, resembled the the Roman empire, while the South approximated the outnumbered Carthaginians in the Third Punic War. Again, her thoughts were more prescient than she could have known.

In her musings about the war and military history, Mary came to see war as a "game of chess." Sadly for the South, it had "an unequal number of pawns to begin with." Expanding her metaphor, she wrote, "We had knights, kings, queens, bishops, and castles enough. But our skillful generals—whenever they cannot arrange the board to suit them exactly, they burn up everything and march away." This was an obvious reference to the surrenders of Fort Donelson, Nashville, and New Orleans.

Mary also commented upon how the string of reverses and the reality of war and death affected people who had never thought about such things previously. She recalled that when European nations became embroiled in fighting, such as during the Crimean

War of 1853–1856, "what did we care?" Now, however, everything was different. As Mary noted all too aptly, "you hear of a battle with a thrill and a shudder. It has come home to us. Half the people that we know in the world are under the enemy's guns."

The comments that Mary made about the war reflected a deeper reality. When the Southern states seceded, everyone treated military preparations, and the prospect of fighting itself, as a lark: a picnic-like atmosphere prevailed. People viewed the conflict in highly romantic terms. War, it appeared, was a game of high drama, but it seemed to entail little sacrifice or bloodshed. The early victories at Fort Sumter and Manassas served merely to reinforce this belief. But defeats, invasion, and battlefield deaths of loved ones sobered many Southerners and caused them to reassess their view of war. Mary observed how, over the course of just a few months, attitudes toward the war and its cost changed: "When you meet people," she noted in the spring of 1862, "sad and sorrowful is the greeting; they press your hand, tears stand in their eyes or roll down their cheeks, as they happen to have more or less self control." For her part, Mary admitted the war had taught her "how it feels to die—I have felt it again and again." She continued:

> For instance. Someone calls out "Albert Sidney Johnston is killed." My heart stands still. I feel no more. I am for so many . . . minutes . . . utterly without sensation of any kind—dead. And then there is that great throb, that keen agony of physical pain— the works are wound up again, the ticking of the clock begins anew, and I take up the burden of life once more.

Someday, Mary concluded, her "feeble heart" would receive such a blow from bad news, that "[it] will be too worn out to make that awakening jar." By the later stages of the war, unfortunately, many Southerners had grown inured to the constant suffering and seemingly endless bloodshed.

THE CONFEDERATE GOVERNMENT IN RICHMOND was not oblivious to the South's waning military fortunes in 1862, nor to the downward spiral of popular morale. Davis commented upon those problems in his February, 1862, inaugural address. He called for more troops, more guns, and more commitment to the Southern cause, but he also admitted that the Confederacy did not have the resources nor the means to obtain those things. Still, something had to be done, and thus Davis and his advisors undertook the huge task of reorganizing the Confederate mobilization effort. He also reshuffled his cabinet in the hopes that new blood in several of those posts (secretary of war and secretary of state, for example) would revitalize the government.

Among Davis's changes was a request for the first ever conscription in American history. The Confederate Congress agreed to the president's proposal, and on April 16, 1862, passed the bill into law. The Conscription Act called for the draft of all able-bodied men between the ages of eighteen and thirty-five. Supplemental legislation granted exemptions to certain individuals (those employed in the war industries, for example), and extended the age range. By 1864, Congress had expanded the draft to include all men between seventeen and fifty.

The reforms of 1862 marked a great departure in the Confederates' drive for independence. In effect, Davis was in the process of creating a large, centralized government. The draft, and other legislation that empowered him to suspend the writ of habeas corpus and declare martial law, seemed, to many Southerners, to destroy the philosophy of state's rights and to trample on individual liberties. Many were shocked by these developments. They argued passionately that Davis was creating the same kind of government and was receiving the same types of powers as his federal counterpart, Abraham Lincoln. In short, Davis was creating a leviathan little different from that from which they had seceded in 1860 and 1861. Others saw the changes for what they were: desperate measures for desperate times. Mary understood the legislation in those terms, noting in her journal, "Conscription means that we are in a tight place." Until that time, "This war was a volunteer business."

While Southerners tried to digest the news of military reverses in the western theater, and while they tried to make sense of conscription and martial law, Federal armies were on the move in Virginia. The Union's renewed advances caused Mary to reflect yet again upon the military situation. She read that former General-in-Chief of Federal armies Winfield Scott argued that the South's military problems were really a reflection of the soldiers' lack of discipline. "[He] says we have elan [and] courage . . . but that we will not submit to discipline," Mary observed. According to Scott, "If [the war] could be done by one wild desperate dash, [the South] would do it. But [Scott] does not think we can stand the long blank months between the acts." The North, on the other hand could "bear discipline," and hence could patiently await final victory. "They can endure forever," Mary noted resignedly, because "losses in battle" amounted to "nothing" for them. She saw clearly that the North's "resources in men and material of war" were "inexhaustible. *And if they see fit,*" Mary concluded, the Yankees "will fight to the bitter end." Her assessments of the Union's strength were well ahead of her time. Few could have seen as early as the late spring and early summer of 1862 just how rich in men and resources the Union was.

The situation in Virginia in the spring of 1862 was serious. The new Federal commander, Major General George B. McClellan, had transported his entire Army of the Potomac, 100,000 strong, to Fort Monroe on the tip of the Virginia peninsula. He planned to move on Richmond from its unprotected rear. Cautiously and slowly, McClellan advanced north and west, from Yorktown to Williamsburg, while the Southern commander, Joseph E. Johnston, carefully pulled back toward Richmond. Davis, worried by Johnston's movements, wondered if Richmond, too, would be besieged. Johnston finally attacked McClellan on May 31, 1862, at Seven Pines. The attack was poorly coordinated and failed to defeat McClellan decisively. But the real importance of the battle lay in the aftermath. Johnston took a shell fragment in the chest which literally knocked him out of action. Faced with the need of a new commander, Davis responded with the best decision of the war. He turned command of the army in Virginia over to his military advisor, General Robert E. Lee. Lee promptly called his subordinates together and developed a plan to defeat McClellan before he could take Richmond. What followed was the Seven Days Campaign, fought from June 25 to July 2, 1862. Although these battles marked the beginning of Lee's fabled reputation, they were not his finest effort. Bad coordination among his subordinates kept Lee and the Confederates from dealing McClellan a knock-out blow. Nevertheless, when the bloody week ended, McClellan was bottled up at Harrison's Landing on the James, and Richmond was saved.

MARY WATCHED THESE MOMENTOUS EVENTS from distant Columbia. James had gone to Richmond on military business, which meant Mary was alone and not terribly happy to be missing out on the excitement. "It is always his luck," she remarked with a touch of envy, "to arrive in the nick of time and be present at a great battle." James did send Mary telegrams to keep her apprised of the developing action. Thus, she was delighted to record on June 29 that "Victory! Victory heads every telegram now." Mary also noted that "For the first time since Joe Johnston was wounded at Seven Pines, we may breathe freely. We were so afraid of another general, or a new one. . . . Now we are throwing up our caps for R. E. Lee."

Lee's success on the Peninsula elevated his status among all Southerners, and especially, Mary Chesnut. Just two weeks before, Mary had recorded reservations about the new commander in her journal. In that entry, she had echoed the complaints of others who had dubbed Lee the "king of spades," because of his orders to dig in around Richmond. "Our chiefs," Mary wrote, "contrive to dampen and destroy the enthusiasm of all who go near them. So much entrenching [as Lee ordered] and falling back destroys the morale of any army." But after Lee's heroics in defense of the Confederate capital, Mary came to regard him as the greatest of the Confederacy's generals.

James Chesnut had always maintained a high opinion of Lee, and this view was vindicated after seeing Lee in action on the Peninsula. James wrote Mary a lengthy letter on June 29 telling her of all that he had witnessed. He noted that the fight at Gaines's Mill on the 27th "was the largest and fiercest of the whole war—some 60,000 or 70,[000] with great preponderance on the side of the enemy. . . . But our men and generals were superior." James went on to describe to Mary some high drama:

Our line by superior numbers and superior artillery impregnably posted, was three times repulsed when Lee, assembling all the generals to the front, told them that victory depended on carrying the batteries and defeating the enemy before them. . . . If night came without victory, all was lost, and that the work must be done by the bayonet. Our men then made a rapid and irresistible charge, without powder, and carried everything. The enemy melted before them and ran with the utmost speed. . . . The field became one dense cloud of smoke, so that nothing could be seen but the incessant flashes of fire through the clouds.

James returned to Columbia about a week after the last of the battles was fought. He noted the distressing tendency of "military jealousy" which seemed to infect the army, and warned Mary of the bad consequences of such gossip. For her part, Mary was disturbed by the long casualty lists—and the death of some friends in the conflict. "Think of all these young lives sacrificed!", she remarked with obvious emotion. She knew that the "best and bravest" of the younger generation was being slowly swept away.

Throughout the spring and summer, while Mary watched the war and recorded the events in her journals, she continued to do volunteer work in local hospitals. Before the end of July, however, she was ill again, caused, she believed, by her hospital duties. Because she could not seem to recuperate fully, Mary journeyed to her sister Kate's summer home in Flat Rock, North Carolina. Both Mary and James hoped that the cooler climate in the mountains and the prospect of total rest and relaxation would allow her to recover completely. Mary complained often about "fevers," and a feeling of a "high steam pressure engine" in her chest. She also wrote to friends that her fevers and chest pains made her "weak & nervous." It is highly probable that Mary, at the age of thirty-nine, was already beginning to suffer from the heart disease that would eventually kill her.

Mary did not allow her ill health to interfere with her correspondence with James or her friends in South Carolina and Richmond. Though she recorded in her journal that "for weeks life was a blank. I remember nothing [because] [t]he illness which had been creeping on for so long . . . took me by the throat," she appears to have recovered sufficiently by August to write to James. She noted that she seemed to be regaining her strength under the watchful eye of her sister. Mary also told James that she had attended church the Sunday before, and that she was able to eat a bland, light diet of "Rice & Milk & lime water & soft peaches." She also assured her husband on several occasions that she was successfully coping with her illness without a resort to opium. Mary, like many others in the nineteenth century, often relied upon narcotics like opium and laudanum. They, she wrote, "quiet my nerves [so] that I can calmly reason & take rational views of things otherwise maddening."

James's position on the executive council in South Carolina troubled Mary a good bit, and undoubtedly helped get her mind off her own ills. She wrote to her friend Charlotte Wigfall that she felt guilty about leaving James "in a hirnet's [sic] nest." From all accounts, popular resentment of the executive council was assuming alarming proportions, and was fueled by Governor Pickens, who resented the encroachments upon his executive privilege. Many called loudly for the termination of the council. Such developments, Mary well-knew, could destroy James's career. She wrote to James that the "Columbia anxieties" bothered her greatly. She noted too that the Columbia papers and certain well-placed politicians "talk of impeaching you for what I think you have done to save your country—putting down distilleries—making arms & ammunition[,] organizing the military, &c &c." Mary went on to write caustically, "I wonder if they thought you would be like [Governor Francis] Pickens—a great old horse fly buzzing & fuming & fretting & doing nothing but hire & bribe newspaper people to write & abuse friends & enemies." She continued to write to James about his sinking political fortunes and warned him that she feared a conspiracy to hurt his career might be afoot. She encouraged him to resign his position and to seek another post in Richmond. As Mary put it, James should "try Jeff Davis awhile."

While Mary rested in Flat Rock, the war rushed on. After successfully defending Richmond, Lee embarked upon an offensive that was designed to ease the pressure on the Confederate capital. He moved his newly christened Army of Northern Virginia Northward toward the old Manassas battlefield. In late August of 1862, Lee's army won a crushing victory over Union Major General John Pope's Army of Virginia.* For her part, Mary was thrilled to learn of the news, though she admitted to Charlotte Wigfall that her refuge in North Carolina "is so beautiful & so peaceful it is hard to remember the storm that is raging with you in Virginia."

Emboldened by his win at Second Manassas, Lee asked Davis to approve an invasion of the North. Both Lee and Davis hoped that a decisive victory North of the Potomac would convince England and France to recognize the Confederacy and thus insure a steady supply of war goods. They also hoped that another victory would attract Maryland, a key border state, to the Confederate standard and break Union morale.

The Confederate army that splashed across the Potomac on September 4, 1862, was in ragged shape. Fully one quarter of the troops were barefoot; their bloody tracks on the hard roads revealed the route they followed. The Confederates' supplies were low, and many men were subsisting on reduced rations. Straggling was also a concern, for thousands of soldiers fell back along the way, too tired or hungry to continue the advance. None of these problems seemed to daunt Lee; he was determined to give Virginia's countryside a respite from fighting and foraging.

Lee's hopes of a grand victory in Maryland were dashed when two Union soldiers found a copy of his orders wrapped around some cigars in an abandoned campsite on September 13. At that juncture, Lee's army was scattered in five different locations. Upon learning that General McClellan (back in command after the Pope's debacle at Second Manassas) knew about the Confederate troop positions, Lee had no choice but to pull together his divided army. He chose to make his stand at the town of Sharpsburg on the banks of Antietam

---

*Pope's new command was composed of armies that had operated unsuccessfully against Stonewall Jackson during Jackson's famed Shenandoah Valley Campaign of 1862. Interestingly, this army was not named after a body of water, as virtually every other Union army was.

Creek. The battle which followed on September 17, 1862, was the bloodiest day of the war: over 23,000 men fell between sunrise and sunset. Although Antietam was tactically a draw, Confederate casualties (which approximated over twenty-five percent of those engaged), forced Lee to withdraw his army South, thus allowing McClellan to claim a tactical victory. This costly triumph of Northern arms was the one for which Lincoln was waiting. He used the occasion to issue his preliminary Emancipation Proclamation on September 22. That document, which was framed as a war measure, stated that on January 1, 1863, all slaves in the rebellious states would be "thenceforward, and forever free."

The Confederate loss at Antietam was a serious one, but Lee had one last chance to end the year on a high note. He withdrew his army to strong fortifications in the hills around Fredericksburg, Virginia, in mid-November. Major General Ambrose Burnside, who succeeded McClellan to high command after McClellan allowed Lee to escape from Antietam, managed to beat Lee in the race for Fredericksburg. But Burnside could not capitalize on his initial success because he lacked the means to cross the Rappahannock River. The War Department failed to send him pontoon boats to help make the crossing. Burnside was forced to watch Lee dig in on the heights above Fredericksburg while he waited for the arrival of the pontoons. When Burnside finally did cross, in December, 1862, Lee was firmly entrenched. Undaunted by the Confederates' formidible position, Burnside ordered suicidal assaults upon the hill. He suffered a bloody, decisive defeat. Southerners ended the year with a momentary feeling of triumph.

While the battle on the Rappahannock raged, Mary and James prepared to leave South Carolina for Richmond. President Davis had rescued James from the "hornet's nest" of South Carolina state government and offered him the post of personal military aide, an offer James had accepted. No one was happier about the appointment than Mary. After being relegated to the relative backwater of Columbia and Camden for most of the year, she was finally going to get her wish of returning to the seat of Confederate power.

Chapter Five

1863:
"Anxiety Pervades"

WHEN MARY AND JAMES CHESNUT ARRIVED in Richmond in late December, 1862, the Confederate capital was still abuzz with talk of Ambrose Burnside's ill-fated attempt to capture Fredericksburg. James's new position in Richmond brought him into the thick of post-Fredericksburg Confederate military affairs. Newly promoted to colonel and working closely with President Jefferson Davis meant that he was where Mary had always hoped he would be. Naturally, she was delighted. For months, she had harbored a deep disappointment that James had been overlooked at the seat of power. His position in South Carolina was an important but thankless one that kept him too far out of the public eye for Mary's liking. Still more ambitious for her husband than he was for himself, Mary found James's renewed visibility gratifying and exciting. He finally had a high profile position within the Confederate government. Moreover, his place on Davis's staff allowed her to be with her close friends Jefferson and Varina Davis, and others within the Confederacy's social and political elite.

The Chesnuts initially took up residence at the Ballard House hotel, but after a short time they moved in "with some 'decayed

ladies' forced by trouble, loss of property, &c to receive boarders."
Mary regarded these accomodations as fairly grim: "A dreadful
refuge of the distressed it was. The house was comfortable and table
good. But you paid the most extravagant price, and you were forced
to assume the patient humility of a poor relation"—a position that
was quite unfamiliar to Mary. Nevertheless, Mary felt that the
excitement of Richmond was worth a few indignities.

Mary and James soon moved to another house that also accepted boarders, and there they occupied the entire first floor,
which consisted of "drawing room, dining room, chamber, and two
servants rooms for Molly and Laurence." Soon, however, the arrival
of friends for a lengthy stay, and the constant influx of visitors
(everyone, Mary noted, "from Mr. President Davis . . . down to the
humblest private" came to call) forced Mary to seek other
accomodations. Before long, the Chesnuts found a rental house for
themselves alone on the corner of Twelfth and Clay Streets, almost
directly across from the Confederate White House.

Mary and James's experience in finding lodgings was fairly
typical for Richmond mid-way through the war. The city, as Mary
noted correctly, was "crowded to suffocation—hardly standing room
left." Richmond had become, by Southern standards, a large urban
area virtually overnight. The government bureaus continued to
attract eager office-seekers, the city's factories offered work for
skilled and unskilled alike, and Richmond's location and importance
(the capital would not be given up to Federal forces without a fight)
made it an attractive place for refugees fleeing the advancing Federal armies. But as the city grew, city resources and facilities began
to fail. Richmond lacked adequate police and fire protection, and its
swelling population—by 1863, over 100,000 people were jammed
within its boundaries—put extreme pressure on limited housing
and food supplies.

Mary was aware of these inconveniences, but they did not
dampen her enthusiasm for life in the capital city. Rather, she
revelled in her return. She was, once again, at the center of power
and activity. Almost every evening she entertained, whether in
cramped rental lodgings or in the more spacious home on Twelfth
and Clay. Mary noted rather blithely that even increasing food costs
did not interfere with her parties. During the early winter and spring

of 1863, "Turkeys were thirty dollars a piece," but James's servant Laurence "kept us plentifully supplied." The Chesnuts also benefited from the full larder Mulberry offered: "We had sent us from home," Mary recorded, "wine, rice, potatoes, hams, eggs, butter, pickles. About once a month a man came on with all that the plantation could furnish us."

Mary's ability to obtain such goods and in such quantities without paying the exorbitant prices charged in local markets was the exception rather than the rule in wartime Richmond. The city, like the rest of the South, was feeling the pinch of inflation and food shortages. In fact, deprivation was rapidly becoming a political issue. To many, the source of these problems was the misguided effort of the Confederacy to finance the war.

FROM THE BEGINNING, THE CONFEDERACY had tried to pay for the war without a resort to taxation. Secretary of the Treasury Christopher Memminger proposed a number of initiatives, but they all stopped short of levying an income or property tax. Instead, Memminger proposed and the Congress enacted bills that raised revenue via foreign loans, the sale of government bonds and notes, and the printing of more Confederate currency. By 1863, these policies had proved utterly inadequate. Prices were rising dramatically: the index of commodity prices was over seven times higher than what it had been in 1861. The situation would continue to deteriorate as the year continued.

Realizing that Confederate fiscal policies were creating runaway inflation, Memminger requested that Congress enact some form of taxes. Congress responded with a tax law in April, 1863, which stunned many Southerners by levying taxes on agricultural goods, profits on the sale of certain commodities, and other items. It also called for incomes to be taxed and stipulated that agricultural producers pay a tax-in-kind on crops and livestock. In general, the 1863 tax law called upon Southerners to make a significant financial sacrifice in the name of Confederate independence.

It was the tax-in-kind that caused the most discontent. "TIK men," as the collectors who traveled throughout the countryside were called, became universally distrusted—and detested. If the farmer or planter refused to pay the ten percent tithe, the agent seized his crops. Southerners believed that abuse and fraud pervaded the system, and in many instances, they were correct. It also appeared that the TIK men operated haphazardly and without proper authority. Those factors served to alienate the people and often led to farmers and planters hoarding or destroying their crops and livestock in order to deprive the government agents. This destruction of food needed for the troops and the growing urban populations exacerbated the shortages and hardship.

Even without faulty monetary and taxation policies, the Confederate economy was in trouble. Successful Union invasions and the occupation of key agricultural areas, not to mention the battles that had been fought on prime farmland (in middle Tennessee and eastern Virginia, for example) meant that food production areas were shrinking. This problem was compounded by the reality that before the war, many Southerners had relied on staple crop agriculture for their livelihood: tobacco and especially cotton were the region's chief crops. To be sure, the majority of Southern farmers and planters were self-sufficient, and most produced corn and other grains for home consumption and for the market. But the loss of the producers of those commodities—the men who owned the farms and plantations—to the Confederate armies hurt Southern agriculture severely. Though their wives and overseers took charge, the absence of the male household head led to a significant reduction in production and output.

Perhaps the most serious cause of deprivation was the breakdown of the South's supply system. Even when food was available, it often failed to reach its destination because of problems with the Confederate railroads. By the mid-point of the war, most major lines were deteriorating at a rapid pace, and the dearth of iron (earmarked for the War Department's Ordnance Bureau) made routine maintenance almost impossible. A solution of dubious merit was to cannibalize the Confederacy's secondary rail lines for their iron. Between worn out rails on the principal routes, the destruction of secondary routes, and the lack of trains to transport the goods, the chances that foodstuffs would reach the armies and the cities was slim indeed. All these factors—transportation problems, invasion, shortage of farm labor—created a shrinking agricultural base and an increase in the number of people who could not forage for themselves.

This situation led to some rather dramatic developments in Richmond and elsewhere in the Confederacy during the spring of 1863. In early April, a group of Richmond women gathered at a local church and marched to Capitol Square in search of food, money, and answers to the question of why they and their families were starving. The group grew to number several hundred (some contemporaries believed the mob swelled into the thousands) as it slowly made its way toward the business district and the city's marketplaces. There, bedlam erupted, as the women and a number of men who had joined them in the mob began looting and pillaging. Governor John Letcher and Mayor Joseph Mayo hurried to the scene, but their words did little to soothe the angry throng. Eventually, President Davis appeared and promised to investigate the problem, but in the next breath he told the rioters that if they did not leave the scene in five minutes, he would have an artillery unit open fire upon them. The crowd dispersed, and relative calm was restored.

That the women had made their point became evident the next day, when the Richmond city council met to discuss how to alleviate the persistent problem of hunger within the capital. The initiatives the council approved were significant. The city leaders called for the establishment of a free city market for the "meritorious" poor. For those in reduced circumstances as a result of inflation and shortages, the council saw to the creation of a city depot where low-cost provisions would be sold.

The Richmond Bread Riot, as it was called, was not an isolated occurrence. Bread riots also broke out in such cities as Atlanta, Georgia, and High Point, North Carolina, during 1863, and leaders in those cities responded much the way they did in Richmond. These outbursts provided tangible evidence that all was not well in the Confederacy, and that significant numbers of people were suffering from a want of food. More ominous still, many of those who were most affected were individuals previously untouched by poverty and hunger. During the course of 1863, the ranks of the sufferers would gradually grow to include large numbers of the middle class.

In fact, one bureaucrat would note that by late 1863, prices had increased over ten times what they had been before the war.

Seemingly oblivious to the bedlam, Mary Chesnut made no mention of the Richmond riot in her journals. This omission is striking, especially since she recorded in detail so many other happenings. Maybe Mary was not aware of the disturbance, though that seems unlikely since she lived barely two blocks away from Capitol Square and had the opportunity daily to talk to government officials—including President Davis—who were involved in quelling the riot. Or perhaps Mary did not talk or write about the bread riot because she had little understanding of it. For someone who dined fairly well every night, and who could garner supplies from her husband's country estate, food shortages were not a pressing problem. Furthermore, as someone with slaves to procure household supplies, Mary was buffered from the vagaries of the daily marketplace. Regardless of the reason, Mary's failure to comment on the riot demonstrated, in another fashion, her privileged station in life. While many in Richmond—and elsewhere—suffered from shortages or literally starved, she and her husband usually enjoyed plenty.

Mary may not have felt the pinch of want in terms of food in 1863, but she could not remain totally oblivious to the changes that were occurring around her. She did notice in mid-1863, for example, that locals were doing increasingly without things that were once considered necessities, such as new clothes. Mary observed that, "We were all in a sadly molting condition. We had come to the end of our good clothes in three years and now our only resource was to turn them upside down or inside out—mending, darning, patching." More distressing still was the realization that the Confederate armies were in a similarly ragged condition. Mary watched as 10,000 Confederate troops marched through downtown Richmond and was struck by what she witnessed: "We had seen nothing like this before," she recorded. "Hitherto, it was only regiments marching, spic and span in their fresh clothes, just from home, on their way to the army." Now, "Such rags and tags—nothing alike—most garments and arms taken from the enemy—such shoes!" Mary found it curious that "They did not seem to know their shabby condition."

Ironically, while the Confederacy lacked food and other necessities, it did not suffer from a want of military hardware. Rather, 1863 marked the South's high point in war manufacturing. This development could hardly have been foreseen in 1861. After all, many Southerners were proud that the region was not an industrial one, since cities and factories were considered "nurseries of abolitionism." But the demands of an increasingly modern war required that the Confederacy obtain arms and ammunition—and the means to manufacture them. The Confederacy succeeded in attaining this goal. Led by the War and Navy Departments, the government established a number of depots and government shops for the manufacture of everything from minie balls to uniforms. The government also offered private manufacturers cash advances, raw materials, and labor as enticements to produce war materiel. The net effect of all this activity was a well-organized manufacturing sector that helped keep Southern soldiers armed and equipped on battlefields from Virginia to Texas.

SOUTHERNERS OUTSIDE THE GOVERNMENT and the factories may have had little sense of the Confederacy's industrial transformation, but they could see the tangible result every time the armies began a new campaign. The spring of 1863 was no different in this regard. Mary and other wealthy Southerners had enjoyed a very lively social life during the winter in Richmond, but warmer temperatures meant a renewal of the fighting.

The Federals had a new commander by the spring of 1863. Major General Joseph Hooker relieved Ambrose Burnside and immediately set about trying to push through Lee's army and advance on Richmond. He came to the same grief as his predecessor. Lee soundly defeated Hooker at the Battle of Chancellorsville, May 1–4, 1863. The campaign brought Mary and other residents of Richmond face to face with the reality of war when General George Stoneman's Federal cavalry, under Hooker's orders, raided Confederate supply lines very close to the city. Mary, attending church, noticed that it was difficult to concentrate on the minister's sermon because of the "rattling of the ammunition wagons, [and] the tramp of the soldiers" just outside.

Mary's concern grew after the service concluded. She journeyed to a neighbor's house to get more information about the raid, but was not reassured by what she learned or saw. According to her neighbor, Mrs. Patton, Federal troopers were only forty miles from the capital. Consequently, local authorities were "mustering in the citizens by the thousands" to defend against the supposedly imminent attack. Mary hurried on to the Confederate White House, where she found a whirl of activity—and more bad news. Varina Davis informed her that Stoneman's raiders were just three miles from the capital. Mary recalled, "I went down on my knees, like a stone." She, Mrs. Davis, and a host of others stayed up all night awaiting news of an assault on the Confederate capital. The next morning, James Chesnut, General Custis Lee, and the president rode off to view the situation. "By eight o'clock," Mary recorded, "the troops from Petersburg came in. And the danger was over." Local authorities had learned their lesson: "They will never strip Richmond of troops this way again. We had a narrow squeeze," Mary concluded, "But we escaped."

Richmond had again avoided attack and capture, but any real rejoicing over Stoneman's repulse and Hooker's defeat was muted by word that Confederate General Stonewall Jackson had died after being shot accidentally by his own men during the battle at Chancellorsville. All over the South, people mourned the loss of Lee's greatest lieutenant. Jackson had assumed heroic proportions in the eyes of most Southerners because of his miraculous ability to cull victory from seemingly hopeless defeat. In campaigns in the Shenandoah Valley and again at Chancellorsville, he had inspired his men to super-human efforts. He would be deeply missed in the campaigns ahead.

Shortly after the battle of Chancellorsville, Mary left Richmond to visit various friends and relatives now scattered by the war. She stopped first in North Carolina, where she was reunited with her sister Kate and Kate's family. Mary then traveled home to South Carolina. It was in Camden that news of her mother's poor health finally reached her. She contacted James immediately, requesting that he dispatch his slave Laurence to accompany her on the long

A Southern woman refugee with all her belongings. Courtesy of Library of Congress.

journey to Alabama and her mother's bedside. James refused, arguing that "It was so hot, the cars so disagreeable—fever would be the inevitable result," and went so far as to forbid Mary from making the trip. Undaunted by her husband's stern reply, Mary went anyway: it was, she believed, her "duty to go to my mother, as I risked nothing but myself."

Mary's decision to make the long, arduous trip to Alabama accompanied only by her maid Molly proved to be a poor one. Problems dogged her from the outset. At one point on the journey, the two women were stranded at a wayside inn with only a drunken man for company. The oppressive heat, the delay of the carriage, and her own ill health combined to make the trip a nightmare. Mary recorded later that, "In my heart I knew my husband was right when he forbade me to undertake this journey."

It was while Mary was en route to Alabama that she learned of devastating news: Vicksburg, the Confederate stronghold on the Mississippi River, had fallen to General Grant on July 4, 1863, after a two-month siege. Mary's reaction to that defeat may have been typical of most Southerners: "I felt a hard blow struck on the top of my head, and my heart took one of its queer turns." "I was," Mary remembered, "utterly unconscious." The Mississippi River was now totally under the control of the Federals, slicing the Confederacy in half. Even the most ardent Confederate supporter regarded this loss as catastrophic in its implications.

But more bad news was to follow. Indeed, as Southerners tried to comprehend the consequences of the loss at Vicksburg, news from the eastern theater slowly filtered south, and the mood grew even more somber. General Lee had hoped that a bold strike north into Pennsylvania would force the Federals to ease their grip on the Mississippi citadel. Further, he felt confident that a victory on Northern soil would crush Northern support for the war effort which might, in turn, force a negotiated peace. Early reports from the field of battle indicated that the Army of Northen Virginia was winning the contest and succeeding in attaining Lee's goals. But gradually, the real situation became known. All dreams of a decisive Confederate victory died on the slopes of Cemetery Ridge at the battle of Gettysburg. Some Southern observers had anticipated such an outcome. Mary noted later that James "was violently opposed to sending our troops into Pennsylvania—wanted all we could spare sent west to make an end there of our enemies [at Vicksburg]."

While Mary was in Alabama, she had the opportunity to observe the attitudes and listen to the sentiments of people in that section of the Confederacy. According to her Uncle William Boykin, patriotism was a limited commodity among the planter elite there. He cynically told Mary that " 'West of the Savannah River it is property first, life next, honor last.' " Mary noted that "Uncle William [says] the men who went into the war to save their negroes are abjectly wretched. Neither side now cares a fig for their beloved negroes— would send them all to hell in a basket . . . to win the fight." As she knew, this marked a decided change in attitude among members of the planter class. That group had, with a few exceptions, supported secession in the hopes that an independent Confederacy would protect their property and their investments. But the reality of war, and the slaves' unwillingness to work for the mistress or the overseer while the master was away, tempered the feelings of many whites in the lower South. Slaves, because of shortages, inflation, and the threat of Union invasion, were becoming more of a burden than a benefit to their owners.

Planter attitudes towards slavery were not the only sentiments that underwent a change during the war. Many, in fact, were beginning to discern an unsavory side to the conflict. Mary noticed that another of her relatives in Alabama, Columbus Haile, confessed he " 'wished we lived in Florida. Easy times, they say, down there.' " Mary countered Haile's assertion by stating, "And yet they are obliged to get substitutes [to fight] there, as you do here. They are making money by blockade-running, cheating the government, and skulking the fight." Haile agreed with Mary's critique, and added, rather tellingly, " 'There are folks such as you describe everywhere. They love to make money and have no stomach for the fight.' "

In general, the disillusionment that Mary witnessed in Alabama was prevalent elsewhere in the Confederacy. Many people in the South were beginning to waver in their support of the Southern cause, especially as problems behind the front lines seemed to worsen and as military reverses increased. Domestic policies such as the tax-in-kind and impressment were still very unpopular on the homefront. A vast number also opposed the year-old draft law, largely because of the exemption system that allowed the owners or overseers of twenty or more slaves to escape military service. Many believed that some were benefiting from the war at the expense of others. Increasingly, the press carried stories about profiteering and editorials against speculation and extortion. By 1863, even the most casual observer could see that the Confederacy was becoming divided along class lines. More ominous still, the Confederate government's initiatives did little to reverse the situation or to allay the common folk's feelings of betrayal. All too often now, one could hear or read about the "rich man's war and the poor man's fight."

MARY'S RETURN TRIP TO RICHMOND WAS PLAGUED by more delays, inadequate riverboat accomodations, and stifling heat. She finally reached Camden by the end of the summer. There she remained until the end of autumn, when she travelled back to Richmond to re-join James.

Mary found the Confederate capital still under the dark pall of the surrender at Vicksburg. The pall would grow heavier as South-ern fortunes continued a seemingly inexorable decline. As always, Mary followed developments closely and confided her thoughts, especially her musings on the military leadership, to her journal. She blamed General Beauregard for the September, 1863 loss of Morris Island, which further threatened the safety of Charleston. According to Mary, Beauregard was "sulking" over being placed in an area of command where he could not enhance his "reputation." She thought General Joseph E. Johnston (sent to Mississippi to rescue Lieutenant General John C. Pemberton and the army be-sieged at Vicksburg) was miffed by Davis's failure to return him to his old command in Virginia. That attitude, Mary assumed, made Johnston less than cooperative when it came time to defend Vicksburg. But Mary reserved her harshest comments for Pemberton, the Pennsylvania-born defender of Vicksburg. For Mary, "[t]hat stupid log of a half-hearted Yankee, lost us Mississippi."

The military situation brightened slightly in mid-September, 1863, when Confederate forces under Braxton Bragg soundly defeated Union General William Rosecrans at the battle of Chickamauga in northern Georgia. But Bragg, stunned by his heavy casualties (he lost over 18,000 men in the two-day battle), failed to follow up on his victory. As Mary recorded, "we looked [for] results that would pay for our losses in battles. . . . Certainly they would capture Rosecrans." She and others in the South were to be disap-pointed—again. "There sits Bragg," Mary wrote with obvious dis-gust, "a good dog howling on his hind legs before Chattanooga." That stalemate would end in November, when Grant lifted the siege of Chattanooga, and pushed Bragg out of Tennessee after the battles of Orchard Knob, Lookout Mountain, and Missionary Ridge. News of the loss of Chattanooga prompted Mary to write: "One begins the day with 'What bad news next, I wonder?' "

James Chesnut had been very active during the entire spring, summer and fall as Davis's military advisor. On several occasions, the president dispatched him to the western armies to assess conditions out there. The Confederate Army of Tennessee had been plagued for months with internal divisions and behind-the-scenes jockeying for preferment with Davis. James, in fact, had remarked to Mary on one occasion that " 'in Johnston's camp and Beauregard's, I was always treated more as a foreign spy than an aide-de-camp of the president of the Confederacy.' " While he tried to mediate conflicts and evaluate the status of the western army, Mary visited relatives or continued her hospital work.

Mary's work at the hospitals exposed her to a side of the war she had hoped to avoid. Despite the horrible sights and sounds, she worked diligently to provide aid and comfort to the increasing numbers of wounded and sick Confederate soldiers who arrived in the city. The Chesnut home on Twelfth and Clay was located across the street from one of the capital's largest hospitals. Although initially disgusted with conditions in the facility, she noted that in 1863 the situation had finally changed for the better. On her "first visit to that tobacco-house hospital," Mary had fainted because the conditions were so primitive. Now, "It was all so neat, clean, comfortable. . . . We [Southerners] have learned," she concluded, "how to do it."

Without question, however, Mary's favorite and most frequent activity when James was away on official business was entertaining. Nothing could dampen her enthusiasm for being with people and hosting parties. She was gratified initially that even James, not normally a socialite, enjoyed the diversions the capital's social scene provided. But Mary remained cautious. James was, "too civil by half. I knew it could not last—going everywhere with us, to parties, to concerts, to private theatricals, even to breakfasts." James soon tired of such frivolity, and stopped accompanying Mary on her outings. On one occasion, Mary reported with a touch of glee, "Mr. Davis came to our relief, and sent the recalcitrant head of our household to inspect . . . the Southern armies generally." Thus began a pattern: Mary would do the majority of her socializing when James was not around to put a damper on the gaiety. She kept a careful accounting of the parties, theatricals, and teas she attended or hosted herself. "Every night," Mary recalled, "our parlor was crammed to its utmost capacity." Even exorbitant prices and persistent shortages did not hamper her revels. Her slave had "simple ideas but effective," Mary noted. " [He says] 'You give me the money, I'll find everything you want.' " Apparently, he did, for Mary believed that most of 1863 represented "days of unmixed pleasure, snatched from the wrath to come."

James's return from the front usually brought an end to the social whirlwind. Mary reported after one of her more notable social successes that "J.C. decides we are to have no more festivities. This is not the time or place for such gaieties." Without reflecting that he may have been right, Mary ignored his orders. She merely waited for James to be called away again on military business, and would then proceed to plan her next party. James knew what went on in his absence and, as Mary observed on more than one occasion, "laid down the law." " 'No more feasting in this house,' " James ordered. " 'This is no time for junketing and merrymaking. There is a positive want of proper feeling in the life you lead.' " Mary would usually respond with a reluctant acceptance that "He is the master of the house—to hear is to obey."

James's criticisms of Mary's levity during a period of Confederate reverses, food shortages, and war-time privation were, in many respects, well-taken. The situation for most people in Richmond and elsewhere in the Confederacy was grim. Loved ones were dying of wounds and disease on distant battlefields, and the majority of families at home were scraping to make ends meet. Mary was not oblivious to these problems, but she, like many, chose to avoid thinking about them. There was in Richmond, and elsewhere in the urban Confederacy, an emphasis on "merrymaking" for those who could afford it. These diversions actually represented the elite's misguided efforts to forget, however momentarily, the harsh reality of the death and destruction that surrounded them. Perhaps not surprisingly, the parties and the revelries would increase as the military situation grew more desperate. It was as if the wealthy sought one more gala event before the world that they knew and loved came crashing down around them.

Many who did not share in the round of parties and theatricals viewed such extravagance with resentment and disgust. John Daniel, editor of the *Richmond Examiner* noted toward the end of 1863 that notwithstanding such gaiety, "The cry of scarcity resounds through the land, raised by the producers in their greed for gain, re-echoed by the consumers in their premature dread of starvation and nakedness." Another resident of Richmond noted rather sadly that "If Spartan austerity is to win our independence, we are a lost nation. I do not like the signs and fear the writing on the wall might in time come to us."

Mary's entertaining proclivities also pointed to another reality. As late as the fall of 1863, she and James continued to be better off financially than most others in the Confederacy. At no time was this more obvious than over the Christmas holidays. Mary's menu for Christmas Day underscores how members of the white elite continued to escape the privations felt by the middle class and poor white members of the population. She noted that "We had for [Christmas] dinner oyster soup, soup a la reine . . . [also] boiled mutton, ham, boned turkey, wild ducks, partridges, plum pudding. Sauterne, burgundy, sherry and Madeira wine." Lee's army in the meantime was subsisting on short rations of bacon and cornmeal, while the average resident of Richmond found the price of a turkey prohibitive. Indeed, when turkey could be had, it was usually a scrawny bird that would barely serve a family of four or five. Mary may have believed that the Chesnuts' sumptuous meal was indicative of "life in the old land yet!", but most others were not so certain.

As 1863 came to an end, many wondered if there would continue to be "life in the old land" in 1864. Military affairs remained rather grim, especially in the West. Davis had finally relieved Bragg as commander of the Army of Tennessee, but he had appointed in his place a man with whom he had been feuding since 1861: Joseph Johnston. On the Virginia front, Lee and George Meade, commander of the Union Army at Gettysburg, were settling into winter quarters along the Rappahannock line. For the Confederates, it would be another long, cold winter.

In Richmond, meanwhile, President Davis was appealing to the Confederate Congress for a revised conscription act that would produce more bodies for the Confederate ranks in the new year. He also asked for the authority to employ free blacks and slaves in noncombat roles. Although Congress continued to criticize the president, it would, in early 1864, pass the legislation he desired. But other domestic problems, especially those dealing with the economy, remained seemingly unsolvable—and largely unaddressed. Inflation continued to spiral, and hardship continued to affect ever greater numbers of the Southern population. It was with a great deal of trepidation that most Southerners greeted the advent of 1864. To be sure, Confederate armies were still in the field, and the Confederate government continued to function. But most everyone could see that the dream of independence was nothing more than an illusion.

Chapter Six

———————————○———————————

1864:
"The Deep Waters Are
Closing Over Us"

THE CHESNUTS BEGAN THE NEW YEAR at their home in Richmond. As was her custom, Mary recorded in her journal the events of the day. But her opening statement betrayed her emotions: "God help my country." The South's prospects were, to say the least, not terribly promising.

Many in the Confederacy were especially disgusted and disenchanted with the actions of the Confederate Congress. President Davis had urged the members to pass legislation to shore up the manpower situation, but the legislature continued to drift. As Mary noted, "Our Congress is so demoralized, so confused, so depressed. They have asked the president, whom they have so hated, so insulted, so crossed and opposed, *prevented* in every way, to speak to them and advise them what to do." Mary continued to defend Davis to all who would listen. But even she noted that the constant strain of dealing with the intransigent lawmakers and the daily reminders of defeat and hardship were taking their toll on the president. His voice, according to Mary contained a "melancholy cadence" of "which he is unconscious . . . as he talks of things as they are now."

Like Davis, Mary could not escape the gloom that seemed to envelop Richmond in the cold days of January. Her journal continued to be the repository of her deepest thoughts and perceptions of the events around her. She noted that Sunday church services were marked by the "anguished" cries of the minister, who begged for deliverance from "battle and murder." Mary observed that all the congregation joined in the fervent prayers, but that by the next day, "we went on as before, hearing of nothing but battle." Mary concluded that most residents of Richmond, like herself "live in a huge barrack. We are shut in, guarded from light without."

CONVERSATION AMONG THE WELL-PLACED in official government circles in 1864 continued to dwell upon the military situation. But for some, including Mary Chesnut, another topic emerged that was both divisive and explosive. That topic was the proposal to arm the slaves and place them in the Confederate army. The plan, proposed secretly by Major General Patrick Cleburne at a January meeting of the general officers in the Army of Tennessee, articulated the idea that many in the South had been contemplating for a long time. Cleburne told his commanding officer, Joseph Johnston, that the South's manpower shortage was growing at an alarming rate; the Confederacy was running out of military-aged men to serve in the ranks. Cleburne suggested that slaves be trained and organized into military units. Those who fought loyally for the Confederacy were to receive their freedom once victory was attained and peace assured. Cleburne's military superiors were divided evenly over the proposal, while many of his civilian chiefs were quite literally stunned by it. When President Davis received word of Cleburne's proposal, he ordered that the plan be suppressed.

In actuality, the idea that the slaves could make an even greater contribution to Southern independence than they did working in war industries or as military teamsters or cooks had been discussed since the very beginning of the war. At that time, most white Southerners had their doubts as to the reliability of black labor. Mary recalled a conversation she had had with a Captain McIlvanie at Mulberry in late 1861. She told McIlvanie that all the South's men were in the army, but after only one year, "we seem at the end of our row. Armies must be recruited." She added that there did not seem to be enough Southern men left to fill the ranks, "unless we put our negroes in our army." Mary rhetorically asked the Captain if "we [could] trust them," but answered her own query in the negative: "'Never.'"

Mary had also overheard a conversation between her father-in-law and a young relative about "black regiments." Old Colonel Chesnut had very definite opinions on that score, and informed the visitor, " 'You can't trust them—not on our side. They won't fight for what they think they are going to have anyhow. They have got it in their heads that this war frees them anyway.' "

White attitudes about arming the slaves changed little as the war progressed. Mary remembered that on the trip to visit her mother in Alabama in 1863, the topic of slaves serving in the army again came up. "General Lee, Mr. Davis, &c, &c—soldiers every-where—want them [slaves] to be put in the army." She related that James and another officer had "discussed the subject one night. Would they fight on our side or desert to the enemy?" Mary believed, as did her husband and his friend, that the slaves "expect to be free anyway," and hence would not fight for the South.

Considering how often the topic of arming slaves had been discussed in the past, Mary found the latest proposal in 1864 a trifle dated. Nonetheless, she continued to follow the course of the debate on Confederate emancipation. Mary noted that many within the South were loathe to consider arming the slaves and placing them in the army. The proposal, Southerners knew, struck at what many believed was the cornerstone of the Confederate nation. By late 1864, that was the crucial issue: would Southerners be willing to sacrifice one of the last vestiges of the antebellum order to attain independence? For many, both within the Confederate government and outside of it, the price of arming the slaves and freeing them once the war was over was too great a one to pay for independence. Confederate Congressman Howell Cobb spoke for many when he stated on the House floor, "The day you make soldiers of them is the beginning of the end of the revolution. If slaves will make good soldiers our whole theory of slavery is wrong." Others went a step further and said that they would rather see the Union Army free the bondsmen—which implied military defeat or conquest—rather than have the Confederate government implement such a policy.

The debate over Cleburne's Memorial would carry over into the final year of the war, and the proposal would continue to elicit strong emotions from all quarters. When General Lee came down on the side of arming the slaves, many in Congress began to relent in their opposition. Still, the final version of the Act to Increase the Military Force of the Confederate States (passed March 13, 1865) was such a watered down version of Cleburne's Memorial that it did not even include the provision to free the slaves in return for their military service. This omission caused Davis to act unilaterally. On March 23, less than a month before Appomatox, he issued an executive order which declared that all slaves who served in the Confederate armies were to be treated as free men. Mary and others realized, however, that Davis's order was "a little too slow" to have any impact on Confederate military fortunes.

EVEN THOUGH LIVING IN RICHMOND WAS like being in "a huge barrack," Mary did not allow the conditions, bad news, nor the debates over arming the slaves to interfere with her social life. If anything, the constant specter of death and destruction led to even more frantic entertaining, with a new twist: weddings became all the rage. She continued to be a frequent guest at the White House of the Confederacy. Mary noted that the number of guests at one of Varina Davis's "luncheon[s] for the ladies" exceeded all other such gatherings. The menu demonstrated that the well-to-do still did not suffer the hardships of the common folk. Mary recorded that the meal consisted of "Gumbo, ducks and olives, supreme de volaille, chickens in jelly, oysters, lettuce salad, chocolate jelly cake, claret soup, [and] champagne." As if that was not enough sustenance for one day, Mary added that "Someone sent us up a supper of terrapin stew, oysters, and Rhine wine, and a box of sugarplums." "I have not," she wrote airily, "the slightest idea who sent it."

Mary's comments about the plenty at the Confederate White House, were natural, especially given the fine repast that was provided. However, such fare, both in quantity and quality, was not typical of the diet of Richmonders—nor of other Southerners—during the winter of 1864. In fact, with increased taxes as a result of the February 1864 tax bill, continued food shortages, and the incessant upward spiral of inflation, most locals were struggling very hard just to survive. Many noted that they subsisted on one or two meals a day; one government bureaucrat remarked that "you take your money to market in the market basket and bring home what you buy in your pocketbook." Another resident of the city stated that his family's income was $600 per month, but that "we are still poor, with flour $300 per barrel; meal, $50 per bushel; and even fresh fish at $5 per pound." As if to underscore how difficult it had become for people to obtain food, a group of concerned citizens met and organized the Richmond Soup Association. Members of the association would visit needy families, and those deemed worthy would receive tickets that entitled them to free soup and bread.

Such socializing in the midst of death and privation deepened the resentment between the various social classes within the Confederacy. Many Southerners, both within Richmond and outside the capital city, grew increasingly critical of, if not hostile to, such gaiety. Phoebe Yates Pember, matron of Richmond's Chimborazo Hospital, wrote during the winter of 1864 that "the city had been unusually gay. Besides parties, private theatricals and tableaux were constantly exhibited. Wise and thoughtful men disapproved of this gayety [sic]." Mrs. Pember noted perceptively that "There is certainly a painful discrepancy between the excitement of dancing and the rumble of ambulances that could be heard in the momentary lull of the music, carrying the wounded to the different hospitals." On a similar note, a woman refugee living in the capital stated more bluntly, "I am mortified to say that there are gay parties given in the city." She went on to add more presciently than she knew that such frivolities were reminiscent of "Paris during the French Revolution, of the 'cholera ball' in Paris, [and] the ball in Brussels the night before the battle of Waterloo." Her comments indicate that almost all classes in the Confederacy were realizing that the flurry of merrymaking marked, in fact, the elite's last gasp. For most observers, there was little difference between Richmond in 1864 and Paris on the eve of the Revolution; nor was there any doubt that the outcome, the destruction of the aristocracy, would be the same. Even

Mary seemed to be in agreement with a friend who "said we could understand the French prisoners in the Reign of Terror now. They danced and flirted until the tumbril came for them, too."

As in the past, Mary's (not to mention the rest of the Southern elite's) seeming indifference to the harsh reality of war angered her husband, and led to what Mary often referred to as a "matrimonial squall." What bothered James most was the reality that his future, not to mention his fortune, was tied up in land and slaves at Mulberry. As the war ground on, James thought it appeared increasingly likely that he and his family would lose everything. Other wealthy Southerners were coming to this same painful realization. Mary recalled that prospect made James subject to "bitter mood[s]" that inevitably led to heated discussions about Mary's frivolous lifestyle. On one occasion, James told Mary that "with so much human misery filling the air—we might stay home and think" about how they were to cope, and what their lives might be like if the South were defeated. Mary's reaction was, as might be expected, rather hostile. "And go mad?" she responded bitterly. "Catch me at it! A yawning—grave—piles of red earth thrown on one side. That is the only future I ever see." Mary admitted that "It is awfully near—that thought of death." But she saw no point in pausing to "stop and think" about it.

Though Mary was perhaps more conscious of the dichotomy between merriment and death and destruction than other members of the upper class, her response was fairly representative. There seemed to be a direct correlation between the number of parties and the tide of Confederate fortunes. As the long days of 1864 grew darker and hope seemed ever dimmer, the number and variety of upper class amusements increased dramatically. Even if food and drink were non-existent, the wealthy would gather at "starvation parties," where they could enjoy some merry-making while they toasted the brave defenders of Richmond with muddy water from the James River. Yet even these supposedly selfless gatherings were suspect, as the elite, including Mary Chesnut, often would eat heartily beforehand so as not to be too ravenous later.

Regardless of the type, parties and celebrations could be found throughout the South in all those areas not yet under Federal control—and even in areas directly threatened by the Federals, such as Charleston and Mobile. As before, the white planter elite was responding to death and hardship much as Mary was: by denying it, or by embracing an attitude of forced gaiety. Mary herself observed at one point in late 1864 that "The deep waters are closing over us. And we are—in this house—like the outsiders at the time of the Flood. . . . We eat, drink, laugh, dance, in lightness of heart," ignoring the horrors that surrounded them. Nonetheless, few could escape the constant funerals and death marches that marked life in the capital and elsewhere in the Confederacy. Nor could they avoid the sight of wounded and maimed soldiers who had come from the front lines to recuperate in local hospitals. Even Mary was forced to admit that "We must sup on death and carnage or go empty."

Still, the misplaced gaiety of the elite, though characterized by its detractors as the norm, was more the exception than the rule in the South from mid-1864. Indeed, most Southerners, including some affluent members of the planter elite, spent their time in much more constructive and productive activities. Mary got a sobering taste of "how the other half " acted when she and the wife of Confederate General John C. Breckinridge "paid our respects to Mrs. [Robert E.] Lee." "Her room," Mary recorded, "was like an industrial school—everyone so busy. Her daughters were all there, plying their needles." Mary was suitably chastened by what she saw. "Did you see how the Lees spend their time!," she remarked to Mrs. Breckinridge. The Lees' activities, as Mary herself admitted guiltily, were a "rebuke" to her own way of handling the impending disaster.

The war, however much Mary tried to ignore it, remained painfully close. During the early winter, Mary recorded that James and the president were called off to inspect fortifications around the city, because Federal raiders were once again coming dangerously near the capital. These developments did not seem to bother her. She noted on occasion that her reading was interrupted by cannon fire, but she did not think it serious enough to flee. "Am I the same poor soul," Mary wondered, "who fell on her knees and prayed and wept and fainted as the first guns boomed from Fort Sumter?" Her laconic response was: "How hardened we grow to war."

Still, Mary was bothered by the implications of the seemingly constant cannonade and the flurry of military activity. Mary, James, President Davis—indeed, almost everyone in Richmond realized that Union raiding parties, not to mention the regular Union army, seemed able to move at will outside the city limits. Mary spoke for most when she noted, "Once more we have repulsed the enemy. But it is humiliating indeed that he can come and threaten us at our very gates whenever he so pleases." "Surely," Mary added, "there is a horrid neglect or mismanagement somewhere!" Actually, it was not so much mismanagement as a lack of manpower. Southerners were becoming increasingly aware that they did not have the necessary numbers of soldiers to protect themselves and their homes against the Yankee invaders.

In mid-March, the Chesnuts received word that James's mother had died at Mulberry. Dutifully, Mary bought mourning clothes, but even that activity brought home how the war had changed the South. Mary wrote that the clothes she obtained "would not have been thought fit for a chambermaid" before the war. Now, however, high prices for material and persistent shortages caused by the Union blockade made people grateful to obtain anything. Mary's rather shabby mourning apparel ultimately cost her over $500.

James was quite affected by his mother's death. All activity at the Chesnut home in Richmond ground to a halt as James went into seclusion to contemplate his loss. His father, frail, blind, and quite elderly, was now alone at Mulberry. Those factors convinced James that he had to return to South Carolina so he could be closer to his father and thus handle the family's affairs. Jefferson Davis aided James's desire by promoting him to brigadier general responsible for organizing and commanding the South Carolina reserves.

As might be expected, Mary was not terribly thrilled about James's decision to return home. She realized, shortly after his promotion to brigadier, that her "busy, happy life" surrounded by "so many friends," was soon to change. Even though that "life" could not last much longer, she was reluctant to return "to that weary, dreary Camden!" Mary's young friends, no more realistic about the future of Richmond than she, were surprised that she was acquiescing to a return to Mulberry—and boredom. One of the Preston girls, who was a regular visitor to the Chesnut household and who was intimately acquainted with Mary's distaste for Camden, stated rather dryly that "Mrs. C's" departure for South Carolina placed her in a position to achieve sainthood.

Mary's impending departure naturally prompted another round of parties. Her days were so busy toward the end of her time in Richmond that she remarked, rather incredibly, "I forgot the affairs of my country utterly." She noted with obvious delight that "My friends in Richmond grieved so that I had to leave them." But, as Mary knew, they did not grieve "half so much, however, as I did."

Once they arrived at Mulberry, the Chesnuts could not help but notice the sadness that seemed to pervade the place after the death of old Mrs. Chesnut. Though the two women had had their share of disagreements in the past, even Mary was moved to note that her mother-in-law "was the good genius of the place." Evidence of old Mrs. Chesnut's "genius" for organizing and tending to Mulberry was everywhere. Mary was struck by how rich the plantation remained, even after three years of war: "Inside, [there were] creature comforts of all kinds—green peas, strawberries, asparagus, spring lamb, spring chickens, fresh eggs, rich yellow butter, clean white linen for one's beds, dazzling white damask for one's table. Such a contrast to Richmond." As Mary well knew, this opulence as late as 1864 stood in stark contrast to most everywhere else in the Confederacy. Because of Mulberry's bounty, Mary wished she could "Bring my houseless, homeless friends who are refugees here to luxuriate in Mulberry's plenty." Soon, however, even this untouched pocket of Southern comfort would be threatened by war and ruin.

Despite being so far removed from the action, the Chesnuts kept abreast of all the military developments. The situation was rather grim for the Confederates. During the winter, the Federal army had been re-organized. Ulysses S. Grant, hero of Vicksburg and Chattanooga, became overall commander of Federal armies. Grant placed William T. Sherman at the helm of the Union's Army of the Tennessee and directed him to move against the Confederate army under Joseph Johnston in north Georgia. Meanwhile, Grant journeyed east to join George G. Meade and the Army of the Potomac. What Grant envisioned—and ordered—was a double offensive against the Confederate armies: Sherman would attack and defeat Johnston, while he squared off against Lee on the Rappahannock–Rapidan line in Virginia.

The dual offensive began in early May, 1864. Grant initiated the action May 4, when he crossed the Rapidan River and headed into an area known as the Wilderness. For the next two days, the armies under Lee and Grant slugged it out. Lee, sensing that Grant would try to outflank him, moved quickly to the South and the pivotal crossroads at Spotsylvania Court House. Once again, the two armies fought a savage, bloody action, and once again, Grant did not allow his heavy casualties—in both battles, he lost over 36,000 men—to stop the offensive. More action—and bloodshed—followed, but on each occasion, Lee was able to parry Grant's blows and keep the Union army from getting between the Confederates and Richmond. Grant almost succeeded in his goal of swinging behind Lee, but the wily Confederate managed to get some troops south of Richmond and in front of Grant before the Federal commander could attack. By mid-June, the two armies had relocated some thirty miles to the south of the Confederate capital, and faced each other in front of Petersburg. What Lee had most feared—and tried to avoid—would now be a reality: he could no longer maneuver in the countryside, but was forced to accept a siege. Lee was well aware that Grant and his legions had the resources of men and materiel to starve him out. Richmond's survival now appeared to be a mere matter of time.

In the West meanwhile, Sherman opened his offensive on May 7, near Dalton, Georgia. His tactics there followed a pattern similar to that which was unfolding in Virginia: Sherman would try to outflank Johnston in order to destroy his railroad lifeline, the Georgia-owned Western & Atlantic Railroad. If Sherman could get behind Johnston and seize the road, the way would be open to Atlanta, the Deep South's chief supply and manufacturing hub. Sherman, however, was unable to outflank the sly Johnston, who answered each of Sherman's moves with a strategic withdrawal that protected his railroad supply line (and thus Atlanta), and his army. By mid-July, that theater, too, seemed to most observers in North and South, hopelessly stalemated.

Mary followed avidly the news of the campaigns and was not reassured by what she read or heard. She noted that Grant's army in Virginia was constantly reinforced, and that Lincoln had directed Grant to "Keep a-peggin." "Now we," Mary remarked, "can only peg out. What have we left of men, &c&c to meet these[?]" She answered her own question with a despairing note that all the South had in the way of able-bodied men were already serving at the front. "Only old men and little boys" were left to be called up to fight. Mary's comments were not idle exaggerations. The reality in 1864 was that all who remained at home were the elderly and the very young, those under seventeen or over fifty, who were exempt from the provisions of the 1864 Conscription Act.

The drama that was unfolding in northern Georgia held a special interest for Mary. During her lengthy stays in Richmond, the Chesnuts had become observers of (and sometimes, participants in) the bitter feud between General Johnston and President Davis. The break began in 1861 when Davis ranked Johnston fourth in order of seniority on a list of full generals in the Confederate army. Johnston, who had been senior to every other Southerner who had resigned his commission to join the Confederate cause and who had held the rank of brigadier general as the Quartermaster General of the United States in 1860, believed he deserved the top spot. Johnston had responded viscerally to the perceived slight; Davis had replied in kind, and a war of words followed by frosty silence ensued. The breach was never mended. Instead, Johnston's exercise of command in 1862 and 1863, and Davis's insistence on micromanaging military operations merely exacerbated the tense association between the two. Relations between Johnston and Davis grew so bitter that even their wives, Lydia Johnston and Varina Davis, were drawn into the dispute.

Acquainted with all the parties involved, Mary developed her own view of the situation. As might be expected, she took the Davises' side, and tended to listen—and believe—those who told her at various times that Johnston was destroying the morale of his army with his constant retreats. She agreed with those who considered Johnston "overcautious." Mary noted, too, that she and her friends in Columbia "agreed that Jeff Davis believed in Joe Johnston's patriotism and loyalty or he would not have placed him, knowing him to be his fiercest enemy personally, in command of the army west." Later, however, Mary would blame Johnston for much that went wrong in the west. "Ignoring his own government has been Joe Johnston's chronic disorder," Mary wrote bitterly after the events of 1864 before Atlanta. "He did not seem to know that he owed any allegiance to our president, because he hated him—and there Joe Johnston's treason to his country came in, and our ruin. . . ." Usually, however, word of army intrigue and jealousies, and the failure to win victories prompted Mary to pray for the leadership of the late Stonewall Jackson if only "for an hour." "We want," Mary would declare, "a hardened fellow who does not value men's lives—only wants to beat . . . Grant and to shunt Sherman aside."

Like other Southerners, Mary tried to live as normal a life as possible while the country she loved entered its most fateful military campaigns. While James conducted his duties among the South Carolina reserves, Mary, with fewer opportunities to socialize, became active again with various benevolent activities. Despite her self-indulgent side, Mary remained, throughout the war, a devoted member of various charitable organizations. Even residence in Richmond did not keep her from staying active with the Camden Ladies' Aid Association. Her return to Mulberry allowed her to resume her role in that organization. She also worked energetically at the Wayside Hospital in Columbia whenever she and James were in residence in that city.

Mary's work at the Wayside Hospital and at the other hospital facilities in Columbia and Camden brought her face to face yet again, with the other, deadly side of the war. Mary recorded in her diary that she assisted in the distribution of food to those soldiers who passed by the Wayside facility. For those too ill or wounded to walk to the food tables, Mary and the other ladies carried "bread and butter, beef, ham [and] . . . hot coffee to them" in the wards. Her exposure to the soldiers who were "awfully smashed up—objects of misery" or who were "maimed" or "diseased" was often too much for her to take. After ministering to those unfortunate men, she usually returned home greatly upset by what she had seen and heard. Mary noted on one occasion that the exposure to the death and disease of the hospital "haunts me all day long—[and] worse at night." There was, she wrote "So much suffering." After another visit, Mary's reaction was somewhat different: "As [soon as] I came into my room I stood on the bare floor and made Ellen undress me and take every thread I had on and throw them all into a wash tub out of doors." It was as if Mary hoped that strong soap and hot water would wash away the horrible sights and smells she witnessed. Still, she was proud of herself for the work she did on a very regular basis: "I am so glad to be a hospital nurse once more. I had excuses enough," she admitted, perhaps aware of past lapses in her hospital service, "but at heart felt a coward and a skulker," when she had declined to help out. "I think I know how men feel who hire a substitute and shirk a fight," Mary remarked soberly. "There must be no dodging duty. It will not do now to send provisions and pay for nurses."

Mary's hospital duties were confined to the morning hours, so she assured herself ample time in the afternoons and evenings for social visits and reading. When not reading novels, Mary could be found eagerly scanning the local papers for war news. Although she was often dismayed by the idiocy and brutality of the war, she could not help being fascinated by it. By summer, she was especially interested in developments that were occurring in the western theater.

Events around Atlanta approached a critical stage by mid-July. Tired of General Johnston's lack of communication with regard to his plans, and fearing he would abandon Atlanta without a fight, Davis replaced Johnston with another friend of Mary's, General John Bell Hood. Without doubt, Hood was a bold and fearless fighter, as he had proved at Gettysburg, where he lost the use of his arm, and at Chickamauga, where he had lost a leg.

Though Hood had won renown as a divisional commander and as an aggressive soldier, he was ill-suited for the command of an entire army. He had lobbied hard for an offensive against Sherman in numerous letters to Davis, letters which also criticized his superior officer, Joseph Johnston. Hood's emphatic declarations about the need to attack made him a prisoner of his own bellicose words once Davis appointed him to command. He had almost no choice but to assault the Federal positions around Atlanta. Hood's offensive produced a series of defeats which forced him to abandon the city. By September 2, the Stars and Stripes flew over Atlanta, and Sherman's army was beginning its occupation.

In some ways, Atlanta's loss was almost anti-climactic. The two armies had jockeyed for position, and the advance had taken so long, that a certain fatalism gripped the spectators. Mary had noted that all knew "The battle is raging for Atlanta—[and] our fate hang[s] in the balance." But in the next breath, she conceded that Atlanta had fallen. "Well—that agony is over. Like David when the child was dead, I will get up from my knees, will wash my face and comb my hair. No hope," Mary concluded, "We will try to have no fear."

After Atlanta's fall, Mary, as well as others in the Confederacy, grew more certain and more pessimistic about the future. Over several months, Southerners had watched as Federal armies moved closer to the Confederate capital and toward one of its major manufacturing centers. They watched as Mobile fell to Admiral Farragut on August 5, and as the Shenandoah Valley, Virginia's bread basket, was ravaged by Federal cavalry throughout the fall. And they viewed with continued alarm the work of the Federal navy as it besieged Charleston and Wilmington, the only two Southern ports that remained open to blockade-running traffic. Many believed as Mary did that there was "No hope." Every piece of bad news "f[e]ll like blows upon a dead body." "Since Atlanta," Mary confessed, "I have felt as if all were dead within me forever."

The loss of Atlanta prompted President Davis to travel west to again confer with the officers of the badly used and mismanaged Army of Tennessee. Davis journeyed first to Hood's headquarters, where he gave the disabled general permission to move his army west and north into Tennessee in the hopes of luring Sherman out of Georgia. After Davis had finished his conference, he proceeded to visit a number of Southern cities—Macon, Augusta, Columbia and Montgomery. Davis's goal on this excursion was two-fold: to encourage the civilian population to keep the faith and make even greater sacrifices, and to convince those Confederate soldiers who had deserted to return to the ranks.

Davis's itinerary included Columbia. Since Mary had rented a small house in the South Carolina capital in early July, she was prevailed upon to entertain the president during his October visit. Naturally, Mary was delighted. He was, after all, an old friend, and his presence would give her the excuse to throw a party. But in planning the dinner, Mary was forced to acknowledge, perhaps for the first time, that hard times in Columbia made it very difficult to set a table worthy of a president. She noted in her journal that as soon as she knew when Davis would arrive, "I began at once to prepare to receive [him] in my small house. His apartments were decorated as well as Confederate stringency would permit. . . . The possibilities were not great, but I did all that could be done for our honored chief." Mary borrowed furniture, drapes, and mirrors from such eminent local families as the Wade Hamptons, and she sent to Mulberry for the Chesnuts' fine china. She remained concerned that dinner, "prepared . . . with only the Confederate commissariat," would be too spartan for such an honored guest. But, the "patriotic public [came] to the rescue." Mary's kitchen was filled with, among other things, "a boned turkey stuffed with truffles, stuffed tomatoes," and a "sixty-year old Madeira from Mulberry."

Davis's visit to Mary's home in Columbia was undoubtedly the highlight of her autumn; in fact, Mary herself regarded it as "one of the pleasantest weeks of my life." She was in her element, and her spirits were lifted with Davis's visit. But with his departure for Richmond, Mary's feelings of melancholy descended again, as did her sense of foreboding. It was during this period that Mary began to refer to herself in her journal and in conversation as "Cassandra," after the daughter of the ancient King of Troy who was cursed by her ability to predict the future, but whose prophecies went unheeded by those around her. Mary's predictions as Cassandra always had an element of doom. Even after hosting what she considered to be her finest party, Mary had feelings of doubt. She confided to her friend Isabella Martin that such feasting and socializing was the "wind-up" of an era. The "old life's" days were numbered and parties allowed them "to die royally."

Mary made little effort to hide her gloomy sentiments. One evening, after she, James, and several others discussed the military situation, Mary remarked that "Tonight Cassandra wails in the beautiful moonlight." One of her companions asked Mary " 'What does Cassandra see that she shudders so?' " Mary replied, "flocks of buzzards swirling round—swooping down—flapping their nasty wings—crowding in a black cloud to pick the carcass of the dead Confederacy."

MARY WAS NOT THE ONLY ONE WHO VOICED Cassandra-like sentiments toward the end of 1864. Many other staunch supporters of the
Confederate war effort grew weary and discouraged. With battlefield
defeats, continued heavy losses, exorbitant prices, and a deteriorating quality of life, it was increasingly obvious that the Confederacy's
days were numbered. More distressing still, the Southern armies
seemed infected with this same sense of defeat and demoralization.
As Mary noted, the prevailing sentiment among the soldiers seemed
to be, " 'Why should we fight and die when it is no use?' And so they
disappear," Mary observed. "They quietly desert at night and slip
away home." Even Mary, fervent Confederate supporter that she
was, began to despair. One particularly candid entry in her journal
recalled how much had changed since the halcyon days of 1861:

> When I remember all the true-hearted, the lighthearted, the gay
> and gallant boys who have come laughing, singing, dancing in my
> way in the three years past, I have looked into their brave young
> eyes and helped them as I could every way and then see them no
> more forever. They lie stark and cold, dead upon the battlefield or
> moldering away in hospitals and prisons—which is worse. I think,
> if I consider the long array of those bright youths and loyal men
> who have gone to their deaths almost before my very eyes, my
> heart might break, too.
>   Is anything worth it? This fearful sacrifice—this awful pen-
> alty we pay for war?

The South's prospects grew dimmer as October turned into
November. Many viewed with interest the North's presidential
contest between Abraham Lincoln and his Democratic opponent,
General George B. McClellan. Southerners were hopeful that peace
sentiment in the North, which grew dramtically as the twin war
theaters bogged down, would force Lincoln out of office—and thus
end the war in a stalemate. But the fall of Atlanta turned the tide,
and Lincoln was handily reelected. Now, as all Southerners knew,
there would be no negotiated settlement unless it stipulated the
return of the South to the United States.

Military affairs did little to brighten Confederate prospects in
the aftermath of Lincoln's reelection. After giving up Atlanta, General Hood's army moved into Alabama and then north into Tennes-

see. Sherman followed him until late October, when he gave up the chase and returned to Atlanta. Hood boldly continued his advance into middle Tennessee, but there his dreams of brilliant victory and an onward march to the Ohio River died. He was soundly defeated at the Battle of Franklin on November 30, and almost lost his army at the Battle of Nashville on December 15–16. Hood's shattered remnants streamed back to Georgia where they would be reorganized under Joseph Johnston in early 1865.

While Hood embarked upon his ill-fated Tennessee campaign, Sherman was set to rewrite the book on military tactics. He ordered Atlanta destroyed in mid-November, severed his supply and communications lines, and divided his army into two wings. What he envisioned was a "March to the Sea," where his army would live off the land and make the civilian population feel the horrors of war. Sherman believed that only by breaking the civilian will, by humbling the people who continued to support and encourage the Confederate armies in the field, would the war be brought to a close. Most Southerners, such as Mary, could only watch as Sherman burned and plundered his way through Georgia. There was no opposition force large enough, strong enough, nor equipped enough to stop the Federal juggernaut. "We are at sea. Our boat has sprung a leak," Mary would write in mid-November as Sherman began his advance toward Savannah and the sea. Few could view the approach of a new year with much hope for the future.

Chapter Seven

———○———

1865:
"The Grand Smash
Has Come"

MARY GREETED 1865 WITH FRIENDS IN COLUMBIA, after bidding a "sad farewell" to Mulberry, "the home," Mary conceded, "that I have always hated. Now I think," she admitted, "perhaps I may have been mistaken. It is a magnificent country seat." The tearful goodbye to Mulberry, however, meant a return to Columbia, and all the excitement on which Mary had always thrived. Columbia, in 1865, was bustling: it was, by that time, one of the largest cities in the Confederacy, crowded with troops and refugees who were all seeking safe haven from Sherman's advancing legions.

The situation was quite critical for the South. Sherman had reached Savannah and had presented it as a "Christmas present" to President Lincoln on December 21, 1864. He stayed in the Georgia port until New Year's Day, when he directed his corps commanders to begin the move north toward Beaufort, South Carolina. Sherman ordered feints toward Charleston and Augusta to deceive the Confederates into believing those cities were his next targets. While Confederate forces scrambled to bolster the defenses of Augusta, a crucial manufacturing center, and Charleston, the venerable blockade-running hub, Sherman set his sights on the lightly defended South Carolina capital.

If Southerners had been dismayed and anguished by Sherman's march through Georgia, they would be horrified even more by his advance into South Carolina. The Federal troops and their steely commander viewed the Palmetto State as the cause of four years of woe. Sherman himself remarked that he trembled for South Carolina; his men were bent on exacting even more justice and inflicting even more ruin than they had in Georgia.

Southerners had little in the way of troops to meet Sherman's threat. The remnants of the Army of Tennessee had straggled back from Hood's disastrous campaign, disorganized and utterly demoralized. Homeguard units and the state militia made some attempt to put up a defense against Sherman's onslaught in both Georgia and South Carolina, but these units of old men and boys were little match for Sherman's crack veterans. Indeed, James had written to Mary that his units of the South Carolina Reserves were "in the main undisciplined, broken down, and . . . comparatively worthless," especially when matched against the Federals.

The cause of such disarray was not hard to find. The Southern fighting men had lost hope and desertions reached epidemic proportions. Mary recalled that a friend told her at dinner one evening that "All the troops from the mountainous parts of South Carolina, and from North Carolina's mountains . . . were disaffected. They wanted peace." Mary had the opportunity to view such actions first-hand not too long after that conversation. She watched out her window and often saw men "passing the *wrong way*. . . . No songs or shouts now," in obvious contrast to the way things had been in 1861. "They have given the thing up."

Accounts from home forced many of the rank and file to slip away from their units. They heard reports of the depredations the Northern invaders committed as they made they made their way through Georgia and into South Carolina. They believed they had no choice but to desert in order to return home to protect their parents, their wives, and their children. Mary saw how powerful the tug of home was when she saw a man arrested for desertion tied up and dragged away—and heard his wife's pleas as he went: " 'Take it easy, Jake—you desert again, quick as you kin—come back to your wife and children.'" As Mary well knew, if the women of the South—once the Confederacy's staunchest boosters and strongest patriots—were encouraging their husbands and sons to leave the fight, the cause was indeed hopeless.

The dawning realization that Confederate forces were evaporating as the enemy approached did little to reassure Mary and others in Sherman's path that they would be protected. It appeared as if the Union army was invading at will; there was little in the way of Southern troops to turn them back. Mary and others could not help be horrified at the prospect. In mid-January, Mary admitted that she had finally succumbed to her worst fears: "Yesterday I broke down— gave way to abject terror. The news of Sherman's advance—and no news of my husband. Today—wrapped up on the sofa—too dismal for moaning, even." Just a short time later, however, she pulled herself together. It was as if continued bad news steeled her for whatever might happen: "I am calm and serene as the moonbeams," Mary wrote. "Such terrible danger steadies me. I never moan or put a shawl over my head now. And I am never ill—no time for that."

Mary's sense of calm would not last long. In early February, she received word that Sherman was advancing not toward Charleston and Augusta as most Southerners supposed, but toward Columbia. James told Mary to pack up and head for the safety of Mulberry, which was about forty miles northeast of Columbia. But after listening to a Tennessee refugee describe "such pictures of the horrors" that Northern invasion brought to her home state, Mary decided no place in South Carolina was safe. With the aid of her slaves, Ellen and Laurence, she packed up what she could and fled. Mary Chesnut now joined the ranks of thousands of other refugee women who were forced from their homes by the invading Union armies.

Mary's diary recorded her horror, outrage, and despair at being forced to leave Columbia, but it also highlighted how broken down Confederate railroads had become. What passenger trains were in service ran late or not at all because of troop needs. Civilians attempting to return to safe havens or flee advancing Union troops had to allow for the vagaries of train travel. Mary, in fact, noted that she and the others with whom she traveled were "detained 12 hours on the road"—a common occurrence by 1865—"and so had to remain a day & night at Charlotte." Because of the delay, Mary decided to stay in her hotel room while she awaited another train. The next day, Mary boarded a train that took her to Lincolnton, North Carolina. She chose that place because if threatened, "I could then run to Richmond or to Columbia or at worst to [her sister Kate's at] Flat Rock."

Without a doubt, the whole experience of fleeing and being forced to choose a new place to live was traumatic for the usually carefree Mary. She was, she wrote, "broken hearted & in Exile." Her surroundings did little to boost her sad spirits: "Such a place! No carpet—a horrid feather bed—soiled sheets—a pine table, &c&c—for this I pay 30 dollars a day." The situation was made all the more intolerable because she had little in the way of food. "The day I left home," she recalled, "I had packed a box of flour, sugar, rice, coffee, &c&c, but my husband would not let me bring it. He said I was coming to a land of plenty. Unexplored North Carolina, where the foot of Yankee marauder was unknown." What she found, however, was that without that box she would "starve."

Mary's experience as a refugee was little different from the thousands of other Confederates who had been forced to leave their homes when the Union army threatened. From the very beginning of the war, Southerners, and especially women, had fled at the approach of Federal troops. Most refugees flocked to cities, but overcrowding, food shortages, and high prices made their relocation anywhere an increasingly difficult venture, especially as Confederate territory shrank in 1864 and 1865. Those individuals forced to flee often sought to cushion the blow by seeking out friends and relatives in other parts of the Confederacy. But even familiar faces did little to ease the pain and loss of being forced to leave one's home.

The refugee population had always caused problems and instability in various areas of the Confederacy. But the tremendous increase in refugee numbers late in the war heightened the chaos and dislocation that marked most areas of the Confederacy by 1865. The appearance of refugees in cities and towns previously untouched by the war also caused increased demoralization among the

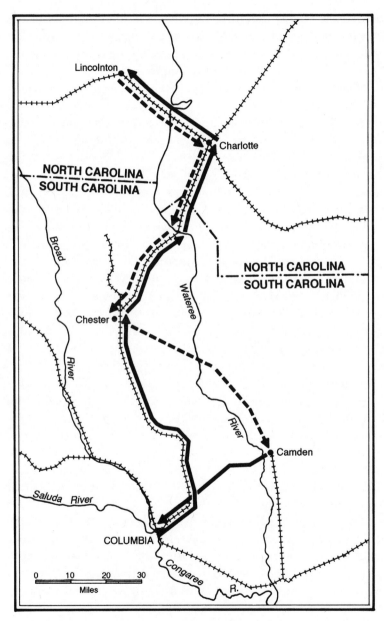

Map of Mary Boykin Chesnut's Route as a refugee, February to
May, 1865.

local residents. Those refugees served as a grim reminder of how dramatically the tide of war had turned against the South. The reality of impending destruction caused Confederate morale and thus support for the war effort to plummet.

Mary's experience as a refugee merely deepened her depression over the ultimate fate of the Southern cause. She noted woefully that her North Carolina benefactors "cannot comprehend the height from which we have fallen." Still, Mary was luckier than most, for through "a Divine providence," she was able to locate a place to live. Her new landlady, Miss McLean, provided Mary with "*my own fireside*—in a clean room, airy and comfortable!" Those new quarters seemed to lessen the sting of being compelled to pay $240 for her four day stay in dingy quarters elsewhere. That exorbitant fee, indeed the whole experience of relocating to Lincolnton, gave her a new perspective on how most Southerners had been living.

Despite new and better surroundings, Mary found cause to complain. She noted that "This mine hostess is young & handsome, very well educated, [and] talks well." Further, Miss McLean was related to some of the first families of North Carolina, including Mrs. "Stonewall" Jackson. Yet according to Mary, she did not "brush her teeth—the first evidence of civilization—& lives amidst *dirt* in a way that would shame the poorest overseer's wife." Mary did admit that Miss McLean appeared a "Lady . . . in manners & taste," but that she lived in "*surroundings* worthy a barbarian." Despite Mary's distress at Miss McLean's indifference to cleanliness, she did realize that she was better off than most other women in her situation. Mary had, after all, a place to stay and food to eat. Because of that, Mary resolved to "love this *N.C.* flower in spite of her growing in this bed of dirt—like a pure white lily."

That Mary would find reason to criticize her benefactor, even in the privacy of a personal journal, after she was rescued from worse surroundings may seem curious. But Mary's comments are not unusual when it is remembered that she had, throughout the conflict, enjoyed a standard of living unknown to most people in the Confederacy. Now, she was totally dependent on others for her well-being and protection. But that reality did not temper her sense of propriety and class status, at least in private. In this respect, she was no different from other wealthy white women who had been forced to flee. They, too, refused to accept that condition as a sign that they had declined in social standing. Mary and many other Southern women were becoming destitute and homeless, but they persisted in drawing distinctions between themselves and others of less exalted status. This insistence upon making such distinctions did not sit well among their poorer benefactors. Those people were not oblivious to the reality that the refugees, however well off they once had been, were now dependent upon their kindnesses. Friction often developed, and class tensions between the rich and poor, which had existed for years, grew even greater.

Mary may have been a refugee, but she was not ignorant of the tide of the war in her home state of South Carolina. Shortly after her arrival in North Carolina, she remarked: "I thought the bitter pang of ruin over—but when I heard yesterday [February 15] that Columbia was attacked—I feel weak & *ill* once more."

Many others would grow "weak and ill" when they learned of Columbia's fate. Sherman's army crossed the Edisto River on February 9 and aimed for Columbia. The Union veterans easily pushed aside the rag-tag Confederate defenders sent to delay their advance. As the Federal army began to shell the capital, locals hurriedly packed up their belongings and fled. On Friday, February 17, Sherman rode into the town and was greeted by the mayor, members of the city council, and a white flag of surrender. In the course of evacuating the city, however, people had carelessly left bales of cotton blocking the major downtown thoroughfares. More worrisome still, government warehouses containing a large quantity of liquor were left open and quickly fell prey to looting Federal soldiers. A careless match, massive amounts of highly flammable whiskey, intoxicated Union troops, and large cotton bales combined to form a deadly mixture. During the night of February 17, fire broke out and quickly swept through the downtown area. Many Union soldiers tried to extinguish the blaze—and round up the suspected arsonists who had started the inferno—but they could not. By the next day, the proud capital of South Carolina was in ashes; more than half of all Columbia's buildings had been destroyed.

Mary learned about the consequences of the Federal assault on Columbia from a friend, who informed her that the South Carolina capital had been "burned to the ground." "I bowed my head and

sobbed aloud," she remembered. Later, after reading a more detailed account of the evacuation and destructive fire in the newspaper, Mary's sentiments altered noticeably. Her tears of sorrow over
Columbia's fate dissolved into shock and outrage:

> The [Union] soldiers tore the bundles of clothes . . . that the poor
> wretches tried to save from their burning houses and dashed
> them back into the flames. . . . They were howling round the fires
> like demons, these Yankees, in their joy and triumph at our
> destruction.

Though she and others were disgusted by the Federals' actions, they
were also devastated at what they implied: the ruin of homes and
fortunes. "I am so utterly heart broken," Mary would write. "Oh my
Heavenly Father look down & pity us." As she and others well knew,
"The grand smash [had] come."

The realization and acceptance that the Confederacy was tee-
tering on the brink of annihilation caused many formerly staunch
supporters to give up the fight, both literally and figuratively. In
many ways, Mary was typical; she had once been the Confederacy's
most ardent defender. Now, however, the situation was "beginning
to be unbearable." ". . .there is the gnawing pain all the same," she
would remark. "What is the good of being here at all? Our world has
gone to destruction." Even seeking comfort in religion seemed to do
little to deaden the pain of impending defeat. When she went to
church, Mary admitted that "My heart wanders, and my mind strays
back to South Carolina." She would add, "My faith fails me. It is too
late. No help for us now—in God or man."

Sherman left the smoldering South Carolina capital and continued on his way north. James, still commanding scattered South
Carolina reserve units, wrote to Mary that "We have been driven like
a wild herd from our country—not [so much] from a want of spirit in
the people or the soldiers as from want of energy and competency in
our commanders." But James still had hope that the "restoration of
Joe Johnston [who was reappointed to the command of what was
left of the Army of Tennessee on February 23], will redound to the
advantage of our cause and the reestablishment of our fortunes!"
James's determined optimism echoed the pronouncements of

Ruins of the South Carolina Capitol Building at Columbia, February 1865. Courtesy of the Library of Congress.

Jefferson Davis and others who still believed that "Sherman will be cut off. Joe Johnston, . . . [and] Beauregard will cut him off." Mary, however, was not as sanguine as her husband and the others who continued to have hopes for victory. "These are not the days of Jericho," she commented tellingly. "Names won't do it—blowing horns does not come to much." She would later ask, "Did we lose by imbecility or because one man cannot fight ten for more than four years?"

Mary's acceptance that defeat was looming conjured up "Wearisome thoughts," for it meant that "late in life we are to begin anew." Recognition of that implied "laborious difficult days ahead" for both Chesnuts.

Actually, those "laborious difficult days" began sooner than she expected. At the end of February, Mary could still report that her refugee quarters continued to be "comfortable," even though they, too, now seemed "dingy" to her. More troubling was the shortage of food. Since local merchants—and her landlord—would not accept Confederate money for provisions, Mary was required to "daily part with my raiment for food." On another day, she wrote in her journal that she had received a "godsend": a friend sent over chicken, "sausages, butter, eggs, [and] preserves." Before that tray of victuals arrived, Mary had confronted the reality of an empty larder. Soon thereafter, she was forced to accept on a regular basis the charity of friends, who offered her provisions as gifts because they realized that she had no money to pay for the food. After years of plenty, Mary Chesnut was now flirting with abject poverty. As if to underscore how poor she had become, Mary recorded in her journal that when she accompanied James to the train station in Lincolnton after his visit in early March, "he gave me his last cent."

While Mary remained in Lincolnton, Sherman was completing his conquest of South Carolina. After torching Columbia, the Union general moved north and east, destroying Confederate installations and private property as he made his way through Camden, Chester, and Cheraw. Sherman's move through the state confounded the Confederate generals sent to stop him. General Johnston confessed that he thought the area through which the Union army moved impenetrable during the winter season. Sherman's troops accomplished this feat with few problems and delays, which led Johnston to conclude that Sherman's army rivalled that of Julius Caesar.

The Federal commander ordered his men not to touch private property while they marched, but when that order was breached, there was no punishment of the offenders. As a result, Sherman's impressive march left tangible reminders of his troops' handiwork. "They say no living thing is found in Sherman's track," Mary observed, "only *chimneys,* little telegraph poles to carry the news of Sherman's army backward." For Sherman, that destruction represented simple justice at work. Both he and his men regarded South Carolina as the cause of the war and all its misery. Consequently, they accepted the responsibilty for their actions. What Sherman and his men envisioned was nothing less than the humbling, if not the destruction, of the proud South Carolina aristocracy. Thereafter, those grandees would never forget the price they paid for secession; they would have glaring reminders in the guise of ruined homes and destroyed fields.

Columbia South Carolina, after Sherman and the fire, February, 1865. Courtesy of the Library of Congress.

Mary's sojourn in North Carolina ended in mid-March, when James wrote to tell her he had secured lodgings for them in Chester, South Carolina. Since Sherman was now en route for North Carolina, it was safe for her to return home. But Mary's return trip to South Carolina was not without difficulty. In fact, the journey merely continued the nightmare she began when she was first forced to flee. "Misfortune dogged us from the outset," Mary wrote. "We broke down [with]in two miles of Charlotte and had to walk that distance," undoubtedly because there were no wagons or coaches to convey the weary passengers to the station. That jaunt, Mary recorded, was "Pretty rough on an invalid barely out of a fever." The whole incident was made worse "by losing an invaluable lace veil, worn because I was too poor to buy a cheaper one." The situation did not improve once she arrived in Charlotte. Supposedly private accomodations James had arranged for her were, in actuality, a "public drawing room, open to all." Exhausted, Mary "barricaded" herself there until morning, when she trudged back to the train station, only to learn the train would be delayed another nine hours. When it finally did arrive, it was crammed to capacity with paroled prisoners. Understandably at her wit's end, Mary was rescued by "a kind mail agent" who took her and a few other women passengers "into his comfortable clean mail car." Despite this kindness, she was weak and ill by the time she finally arrived at the station in Chester.

Relocating to Chester reunited Mary with James, and assured her, at least temporarily, of a safe haven that was "fresh, clean, warm, comfortable," and where "We are among the civilized of the earth once more." But Chester did not represent a return of tranquility. Mary's diary indicates that she often lapsed back into her role as Cassandra. She noted that General Stephen D. Lee's army corps marched through Chester on its way to reenforce Johnston in North Carolina. But she believed that the troops were marching "only to surrender." "There they go, the gay and gallant few," Mary wrote. Such a movement, however, was useless: those young men were "doomed." For Mary, their march was doubly sad because it represented "the last gathering of the flower of Southern youth. . . . They continue to prance by—lightly and jauntily," Mary noticed. "They march with as airy a tread as if they believed the world was all on their side—and that there were no Yankee bullets for the unwary." "What," Mary asked, "will Joe Johnston do with them now?"

Mary's sense of helplessness was felt by all Southerners. The impression that the end was fast approaching deepened dramatically as March drew to a close. Lee, boxed in at Petersburg since June, 1864, tried one last attempt to break through Grant's tight cordon. He attacked at Fort Stedman in the Petersburg defenses on March 25, 1865, but was repulsed. The Confederate failure compelled Grant to try to swing south in order to cut Lee off from his remaining railroad link. Success at Five Forks on April 1 led Grant to order an all-out assault against the Petersburg lines the next day. That attack succeeded in crushing the Confederate right. Lee, sensing the danger, had no choice but to pull out of the trenches. His withdrawal from Petersburg meant that Richmond would have to be evacuated.

The evacuation of Richmond on the night of April 2 was a nightmare of confusion. Intent on destroying whatever was of value in the city to prevent it from falling into the hands of the approaching Federals, locals set fire to stores, warehouses, and Confederate depots. As explosions ripped through the city, government officials, townspeople, and military commanders all tried to carry off whatever documents, personal belongings, and war materiel they could. Soldiers and civilians torched cotton and tobacco, and split open barrels of liquor which were then poured into the streets. The combination of liquor, fire, and panic proved costly. Drunken mobs of locals, escaped prisoners, deserters, and former slaves ravaged the city. The blackened sky above the James River told the tale: Richmond was engulfed in flames.

Word that the proud capital of the Confederacy had been abandoned did not reach Mary until five days later. "Richmond has fallen," she would record, "and I have no heart to write about it." She went on to add: "they [the Union troops] are too many for us. Everything lost in Richmond, even our archives. Blue black is our horizon."

The loss of Richmond was a tremendous blow to the Confederacy, materially and psychologically. The capital represented the political heart and economic soul of the Confederate nation. Now, it lay in ruins. President Davis exhorted Southerners to keep the faith, and promised to re-establish the government in another, safer location. The Confederate Congress and President Davis did make their way to Danville, Virginia, where the government briefly reconvened. But that meeting in the small tobacco manufacturing center was the last. Once adjourned, the President and the Congress scattered and sought to save themselves from Federal capture.

Many other Confederate officials and their families crowded the trains heading south and west ahead of the Federal advance. Mary's lodgings in Chester were soon crammed with Southern dignitaries, including Louis Wigfall, John Bell Hood, and Varina Davis, as they hurried to places as varied as Texas, Mexico, and Brazil. The arrival of those friends served only to underscore how desperate the situation had become. Mary noted in mid-April that since she had recorded Richmond's fall in her diary, she had spent a week of "madness, sadness, anxiety, turmoil, [and] ceaseless excitement," as refugees swarmed to the safe haven the Chesnuts' cottage offered. "Night and day," Mary would note, "this landing and these steps [in their rented rooms] are crowded with the elite of the Confederacy going and coming. And when night comes, or rather bedtime, more beds are made on the floor of the landing place, for the war-worn soldiers to rest upon. The whole house is a bivouac."

The turmoil of the past several months had its share of poignant moments that brought home to Mary the horrors of war. She remembered a time once before when General Hood had sought refuge with the Chesnuts. But then as now, the ill-fated general seemed enveloped in sadness. "He [Hood] did not hear a word," Mary recalled telling a friend of the trauma he had endured:

> He had forgotten us all. Did you notice how he stared in the fire? And the livid spots which came out on his face and the huge drops of perspiration that stood out on his forehead? Yes, he is going over some bitter hour. . . . He feels the panic at Nashville . . . And the dead on the battlefield at Franklin. . . .

The reality of old friends forced to flee to safety depressed Mary greatly. One afternoon, while calmly lying on a sofa, the strains of military music must have conjured up memories too painful to bear. "I sprang onto the floor as if I was shot and gave a howl of agony worthy of an Irish wake." One of Mary's guests, alarmed at her reaction, asked, " 'What is the matter? . . . You are crying as if your heart would break.' " " 'Leave her alone,' " answered her friend, Isabella Martin. " 'Let her have her cry out. She has hardly been in her right mind since Sherman left Atlanta behind him.' "

The arrival of the dispossessed and the general turmoil at Mary's refuge in Chester would only increase as the days passed. Then, on April 19, the throng of transients was stunned to learn of Lee's surrender to Grant on April 9 at Appomattox Court House some sixty miles west of Petersburg. Though Mary and the others were shocked and saddened to learn of the capitulation, they still had hopes that Johnston and his tiny force of Confederates in North Carolina could hold out. But those dreams, too, were dashed with word that Johnston, surrounded by a vastly superior enemy, surrendered to Sherman at Bentonville, North Carolina, on April 26.

With the end of fighting and the collapse of the Confederacy, some Southerners took to the roads to avoid capture and arrest at the hands of the Federal army. But for most, including Mary Chesnut, further flight was pointless: "We are going to stay. Running is useless now," she decided. "Why fly? They are everywhere, these Yankees—like red ants—like the locusts and frogs which were the plagues of Egypt."

News of the surrender did not cause a resumption of normal life at the Chesnut's lodgings in Chester. If anything, chaos continued to reign. James was still in command of scattered South Carolina forces, so members of his staff and other high ranking Confederate officers continued to "gallop around with messages." Yankee raids added to the general confusion, and forced Mary, on one occasion, to bury her journals and other valuables. Everywhere, it seemed, were the "yankees hanging over us like the sword of Damocles." In the midst of this confusion, Mary received a dispatch meant for her husband that brought more bad news: Lincoln had been assassinated and Secretary of State William Seward had been badly wounded in a related attempt. All those gathered at the Chesnuts' quarters were certain that the Northern authorities would blame Southerners and "take vengeance on us, now that we are ruined and cannot repel them any longer."

The Chesnuts and their friends remained in the rented rooms until May 2, when Mary and James packed up what belongings they had and started for Camden and Mulberry. As they headed south on their return, Mary was shocked by the devastation they witnessed: "One can never exaggerate the horrors of war on one's own soil," she wrote. "You understate the agony, strive as you will to speak, the agony of the heart—mind—body." She went on to note that, "Since we left Chester—solitude. Nothing but tall blackened chimneys to show that any man has ever trod this road before us. This is Sherman's track. It is hard not to curse him." "I wept incessantly at first," she admitted, especially when she saw the extent of the devastation. James tried to reassure her by pointing out that "The roses of [the] gardens are already hiding the ruins . . . Nature is a wonderful renovator." Mary was not comforted. "I shut my eyes and made a vow," she recorded. "If we are a crushed people, crushed by aught, I have vowed never to be a whimpering pining slave."

The Chesnuts made their way to Mulberry, but that journey only served to remind them that they had lost everything. They could not even scrape together the ten-cent ferry toll to cross the Wateree River to Mulberry. Their arrival at the plantation brought mixed emotions. Though the house was still standing, it had suffered at the hands of the invaders. "On one side of the house," Mary reported, "every window was broken, every bell torn down, every piece of furniture destroyed, every door smashed in. The other side intact." Federal raiders had also destroyed Mulberry's mills, cotton gin, and virtually all of the cotton that had been stored there for future sale. As if that were not enough, the Union troops had ransacked the house and scattered the Chesnuts' precious books and papers all around the yard, though "Somebody said they found some of them as far away as Vance's Ferry." ["Nothing] is left now," Mary concluded, "but the bare land and *debts* made for the support of these hundreds of negroes during the war."

Mulberry may have been a shell of its former grandeur, but it was still home to Mary and James—and to the host of relatives who converged on the old estate. James's father, Colonel Chesnut, was, according to Mary, "in a deplorable state, blind—feeble—fretful—miserable." But at ninety-three, he was still the patriarch of the family. Indeed, Colonel Chesnut was, as Mary wrote, "of a species that we will see no more." He epitomized "The last of the lordly planters who ruled this Southern world." Yet, as Mary and all Southerners knew well, that world—of plantations, and cotton, and slaves—was no more. Perhaps it was fitting that Colonel Chesnut resembled the postwar South. He was, Mary concluded, "a splendid wreck."

The realization that all was indeed lost caused James Chesnut to become withdrawn and bitter. Mary noted that he berated himself for not returning to Mulberry a year sooner "and saving his property as *some* did." Mary, however, thought differently: "I said he did right to lose it." She went on to tell him that "I think still, as you aided in bringing on this war—you were bound to sacrifice all & stick to it no matter where you were placed, no matter how unpleasant your position—for the poor conscripts had to stay in a worse place." James responded that he had stayed in the army "from his 'own conviction of duty'—and not from my persuasion." Mary conceded that this was the case, but she added that James seemed to delight in "taunting" her with "his *ruin*—for which I am no more responsible than the man in the moon." She concluded that "it is a habit of all men to fancy that in some inscrutable way their wives are the cause of all the evil in their lives."

Mary tried to escape the dreariness that surrounded Mulberry by going into Camden, but even that distraction brought only sadness. "There is a monotony in Yankee insolence & wickedness," she recorded on May 10, 1865, "that makes me weary. . . . I am no longer greeted with a thousand smiles. . . . My day in Camden is over. The Yankee dynasty begins to reign." The reality that they were now in occupied territory and that they had lost everything, from material goods to their civil rights as citizens, unnerved Mary. She recorded shortly after her visit to town that "I had a violent fit of hysterics. JC called [to me], shut the door, & seized me—frightened to death—soothing me as if I was dying." "I was ill enough," Mary admitted, "& *wish I had died.*"

The Chesnuts' reactions to the loss of their personal fortunes and the reality of the new, postwar order were understandable. Similar scenes were played out all over the South in the aftermath of the surrender. For their entire lives, these people had enjoyed the very best that money could buy. They had servants who catered to their every whim; they had access to many and varied entertainments; they were surrounded by the finer things of life. They gambled everything and lost. With the Confederacy's defeat, they, along with virtually all white Southerners, were brought face to face with ruin. They had difficulty comprehending how far they had fallen—and how much they had lost. Mary would articulate the unspoken feelings of her family—and other wealthy Southern families who suffered similar fates—when she wrote in her diary: "I can not bear to write the horrible details of our degradation. . . . I thank God that I am *old*—& can not have my life so much longer embittered by this agony." She was forty-three years old when she penned those words.

Chapter Eight

"Cry Aloud for All That is Past & Gone"

THE SURRENDER OF THE CONFEDERATE ARMIES marked the end of one era in Southern history and the beginning of another. The South suffered severely during the course of the war. In 1865, as Southern families such as the Chesnuts made their way back to their homes, they could not help notice the devastation. As Mary remarked, those who retraced Sherman's path were especially discouraged: they saw nothing but gutted houses, burned out shells of factories, and twisted metal of what had been railroads.

War had been cruel to the South. Indeed, there were very few areas within the 750,000 square miles of Confederate territory that remained untouched by the war. Once prosperous cities such as Richmond, Atlanta, Columbia, and Charleston, were in smoldering ruins. Some of the country's richest farmland was now a blasted battlefield landscape. The Confederate nation's recently developed industrial centers were wastelands. Finally, the entire Southern system of labor—and race relations—was in complete disarray because of emancipation. The war also had a high human cost. As Mary had written almost a year before the end, the "flower" of Southern youth were gone; over twenty-five percent of men between the ages of eighteen and forty never returned home. Total Confederate war dead exceeded 260,000, and the numbers of wounded and disabled from the war almost equaled that figure.

Other statistics told equally dismal tales. Land values in the South in the spring of 1865 had declined precipitously, to less than half of what they had been at the war's beginning. Farm property values, too, had fallen well below 1860 figures: they were down almost seventy percent. Over thirty percent of the region's horses, mules, and hogs had been killed, and the loss of draft animals in particular threatened the harvest of spring crops. Southern capital losses were also staggering: it was estimated that over $500 million in gold had been sunk into Confederate notes that were now worthless. Finally, the emancipation of the slaves represented a loss in personal property of almost $3 billion, a figure which represents the largest expropriation of private property in United States history. Many white Southerners could not comprehend the extent of the damage—nor the extent of their personal losses. To add to their woes was the reality of military occupation; the presence of the Union army was a daily reminder that they had fought and lost to a superior foe.

The national mood in the days following the Confederate surrender was mixed. In both sections of the country, people struggled to comprehend just what had happened. In the North, people were divided in sentiment. Some believed that a return to peace should be accomplished with a minimum of upheaval. Others wanted vengeance, especially in the aftermath of Lincoln's assassination. In the South, different emotions dominated. Some former Confederates continued to be outspokenly defiant of "Yankee" domination. Others were too shocked to do much of anything but submit meekly to Federal authorities.

Mary Chesnut's diary entries during those unsettled days mirrored the attitudes of most Southerners. She wrote in mid-May, 1865: "We are scattered—stunned—the remnant of heart left us, filled with brotherly hate." On another occasion, Mary noted that "A feeling of sadness hovers over me now, day and night, that no words of mine can express." Her sentiments changed little over the next two months. By late July, she would remark that her diary, once a

Women Mourners Among the Ruins of Richmond, April, 1865.
Courtesy of the Massachusetts Commandery, Military Order of
the Loyal Legion and the U.S. Army Military History Institute.

source of pleasure, did little to alleviate her pain and despair. "I do
not write often now," Mary recorded, "not for want of something to
say, but from a loathing of all I see and hear. Why dwell on it?"

While Southerners attempted to come to terms with defeat and
devastation, politicians in the North were trying to figure out how to
deal with the economic and political Reconstruction of the South.
The situation in Washington was quite unsettled. The nation was
still in mourning for Abraham Lincoln. Moreover, many of the
country's political leaders were divided over how to deal with the
problem of Reconstruction. People such as the Chesnuts could only
sit and watch as others wrestled with their fate.

ACTUALLY, THE WHOLE PROCESS OF RECONSTRUCTION had begun during the war. In December, 1863, President Lincoln had issued a Proclamation of Amnesty and Reconstruction. That document promised any Southerner a full pardon and the restoration of property in return for an oath of future allegiance to the United States. The proclamation, however, excluded all high-ranking Confederate officials—officers of any rank above colonel and all civil and diplomatic office-holders—from its otherwise generous terms. As further incentive to the South, Lincoln also detailed what came to be known as the "Ten Percent Plan." Whenever ten percent of those people in a particular Southern state who had voted in the 1860 presidential election took the oath of allegiance to the Federal government, that state could proceed to reorganize a government for readmission to the Union. The plan was designed to hasten the restoration process and to insure that loyal Southerners themselves undertook the process of Reconstruction. Lincoln oversaw the implementation of this plan in those areas that were under Federal control during the war: Tennessee, and parts of Virginia, Arkansas, Mississippi, and Louisiana.

Lincoln's plan was a moderate one and was based on the long-held idea that secession had never legally occurred. It was not, however, without its critics. Radical Republicans in the Congress believed that the Southern people should be punished for secession and the war. They urged that a harsh, victor's peace be imposed. Radicals such as Charles Sumner argued that Southerners had committed political suicide when they had taken their states out of the Union. Because of that, the Radicals contended, the Southern states should be treated as "conquered provinces" which would make them subject to congressional regulations. They countered Lincoln's proposal with one of their own in July, 1864. The Wade-Davis Bill, as the Radical proposal was called, required fifty percent of a Southern state's population to take the loyalty oath before a state government could be organized. Further, only those who took an "ironclad oath"—a Southerner had to swear that he had never voluntarily supported the Confederacy during the war—could vote. Some Radicals also called for the redistribution of confiscated land to the freedmen, and they contemplated the possibility of black suffrage.

Lincoln could not accept the harsher Radical proposal, but he also could not accept the divisions within his party and his government over the terms of Reconstruction—especially since the war was still raging. Thus, Lincoln disposed of the Wade-Davis Bill with a pocket veto; the bill died without his signature at the close of the 1864 congressional session.

The issues of how the states should be readmitted and who should direct the process remained pivotal ones to the end of the war. Lincoln assumed that his goal of a fair Reconstruction would be implemented, and he called for as much in his second inaugural address. Obviously, he did not expect an assassin's bullet to interfere with his grand design.

The succession of Andrew Johnson to the presidency on April 15, 1865, changed the equation dramatically. Lincoln had chosen the Democrat from east Tennessee as his running mate in 1864 in order to attract Southern Unionists, as well as War Democrats, and moderate Republicans, to the newly-christened National Union ticket. Lincoln and Johnson ran on a platform pledged to unconditional Southern surrender, a constitutional amendment that formalized emancipation throughout the South, and a continuation of Lincoln's war measures.

The man Lincoln picked in 1864 was a complex individual. Born into a poor family, Andrew Johnson's early life was marked by struggle and hardship. He worked as a tailor in his youth, and married a schoolteacher who eventually taught him to read and write. Entry into politics followed his marriage, and he succeeded in moving up the ladder of political offices. Hard work and financial and political success allowed Johnson to attain a comfortable standard of living which permitted him to become a landholder and slaveholder. Still, despite all his success, Johnson never forgot his humble origins; rather, he remained proud of them to the end of his life.

Johnson had earned the respect of many Republicans, especially the Radicals, during his service as wartime governor of Union-occupied Tennessee. During his term in office, he delighted the Radicals with his strong pronouncements and harsher actions against the Southern aristocracy. Believing that "treason must be made odious," Johnson worked to punish the rebels. He firmly believed

Richmond after the fires, 1865. Courtesy of the Massachusetts Commandery, Military Order of the Loyal Legion and the U.S. Army Military History Institute.

that the planter class had forced secession upon the unwilling majority of yeomen farmers. That act had caused all the South's woes. For Johnson, it seemed only right that the "purse-proud" aristocrats be humbled.

Given Johnson's wartime pronouncements, the Radicals had nothing but fond hopes that their dreams of a punitive peace would be realized. They did not appreciate, however, that Johnson, being the good Jacksonian that he was, hated the monied commercial and industrial elite of the Northern states every bit as much as he did the wealthy Southern planter class. Johnson also rejected the Radicals' views of racial equality. He had been a slaveholder himself and still believed in black inferiority. Thus, the stage was set for a rather heated exchange between the president and the Congress over who should dictate Reconstruction and how it should be accomplished.

Johnson opened the debate May 29, 1865, when he issued his proclamations detailing the requirements Southerners had to fulfill in order to attain a pardon and have their confiscated property returned to them. Basically, these documents reiterated the terms

Lincoln had set down in 1863, but the section dealing with pardons added a significant provision: it denied pardons to all Southerners whose taxable property was worth $20,000 or more. If those Southerners wanted a pardon, they had to apply to Johnson in person. This insured that Johnson would have the opportunity to witness the humbling of the Southern aristocrats he hated most.

The president's proclamations also established what would become the formula for reorganizing and readmitting the loyal governments. Only those Southerners who took the oath of allegiance and who had received a pardon could participate in the creation of the new state governments. Johnson detailed the minimum preconditions the states had to accept in order to be readmitted to the Union. According to his plan, each state had to repudiate the Confederate debt, nullify the ordinance of secession, and recognize the emancipation of the slaves. Once those provisions had been met, the states could proceed to elect representatives to the national Congress and the Reconstruction process would be complete. The Johnson program implied that native white Southerners, and in particular, antebellum Unionists, would play the key roles in the new loyal governments.

SOUTHERNERS WATCHED ALL THESE DEVELOPMENTS with great interest, but in many ways, those who were not covered by the amnesty proclamation were powerless to do anything. Mary Chesnut followed the saga, and as might be expected, commented upon the initial phases of the Reconstruction process in her journal. She wrote in mid-May, "We sit and wait until the drunken tailor [Johnson] who rules the U.S.A. issues a proclamation and defines our anomalous position." Mary's views—and the views of other Southerners in a like situation—changed little after Johnson issued his amnesty acts. She recorded in her diary on June 10, 1865: "Andy Johnson is bloody *minded*—his proclamation allows nobody over the rank of colonel to take the amnesty oath—& nobody who has assisted Confederates who owns over twenty thousand dollars. So ye poor rich men. Ye may now howl." Just two days later, Mary noted with disgust that the Lincoln–Johnson Reconstruction plans elicited "terror." "Destruction to the wealthy classes—it seems highly approved [in the] North by all." "At the South," she added, it was accepted "by all whose property is under [$]20,000."

Mary may have been disgusted and dismayed by the amnesty proclamation, but she was more worried about James's fate. Since he had been a high ranking Confederate military official and owned property worth more than $20,000, he was not covered by the May amnesty act. She observed that former Confederate Congressman and General Howell Cobb, whose service and financial standing paralleled James's, had been arrested. Because of this, Mary expected that "JC may look for his arrest any day." Mary watched James closely to see if he was worried or frightened about his probable arrest and trial for treason, but she could not discern any change in his demeanor. He seemed unmoved by what fate might hold for him. Mary noted that James would not "hide nor fly. He has done nothing he is ashamed of or that he had not a right to do." To demonstrate how unconcerned he was, he sat passively, "calmly read[ing] Macauley." Mary, however, was not quite so calm or unmoved. She considered herself "the Wife of Damocles—for the sword seems suspended by a glittering hair—ready to fall and crush me."

James was not arrested, and applied to be pardoned for his role in the war. In fact, many prominent Southerners whose social status and wartime careers resembled James's found themselves the beneficiaries of Johnson's increasingly generous pardon policies. That lenience, couple with continued Southern defiance, created a rift between the president and the Congress over the future of Reconstruction.

ANDREW JOHNSON'S DESIRE TO COMPLETE the Reconstruction process as quickly as possible fell afoul of Southern actions and Radical desires. Many of the states Johnson had restored to the Union refused to follow the terms he set down. For example, some states repealed the secession ordinance instead of nullifying it. Other states, including South Carolina, also refused to repudiate the Confederate debt for fear it would hurt their attempts to obtain outside credit for economic rebuilding. Finally, some states refused to recognize the emancipation of the slaves, even though it had been formalized with the ratification of the Thirteenth Amendment in 1865.

The members of Congress who reconvened in December, 1865 (Congress was not in session between May and December, and Johnson did not call a special session), were aware that many former Confederate officers and politicians—including Alexander Stephens, former vice president of the Confederacy—had been elected to represent the "reconstructed" South in the Senate and House. To prevent this from occurring, Northern members of Congress pointed to their constitutional right to establish credentials for members of Congress and refused to recognize the newly elected Southern representatives in either chamber. Shortly thereafter, Congress appointed a fifteen-member (nine from the House and six from the Senate) Joint Committee on Reconstruction to investigate how the process of Reconstruction could best be accomplished.

The joint committee established by Congress was dominated by moderates. After hearing testimony, however, from freedmen, Union army officers, and Freedmen's Bureau officials about Black Codes (laws that were designed to insure an agricultural labor force but which actually produced de facto slavery), increased racial violence, and intransigent Southern whites, most of those moderates found themselves becoming more receptive to the overtures of the Radical Republican camp. It would be President Johnson's actions on key pieces of Reconstruction legislation, however, that would make most Republican moderates openly join forces with the Radicals.

Johnson's handling of the readmission of the states irritated members of Congress, but it was his veto of the 1866 Civil Rights Bill and a bill that called for the extension of the Freedmen's Bureau that caused the irreparable break between the president and the Congress. A Republican landslide in the 1866 midterm elections gave the Radicals the numbers they needed to take control of the Reconstruction process. They accomplished this in 1867, when they passed the Military Reconstruction Acts. Those acts divided the South into five military districts and placed each under military rule. The military governors, who were major generals in the United States army, were to oversee the registration of black voters and to help in the re-organization of state governments. Ex-Confederate states could be readmitted to the Union only after they had ratified the Fourteenth Amendment (which called for, among other things, equality under the law, and which was a reformulation of the 1866 Civil Rights bill that was eventually passed over Johnson's veto), elected "loyal" men to state offices, registered the freedmen to vote, and had rewritten their state constitutions. Since virtually every ex-Confederate was disfranchised under the Military Reconstruction Acts, only "Carpetbaggers," Northern Republicans who had moved South, "Scalawags," Southerners who supported the Radical regimes, and free blacks were involved in the process. Most Southern whites would find this policy repugnant, especially since it sought to involve their ex-slaves in the work of restoration.

THOUGH POLITICS REMAINED TURBULENT, Southerners such as Mary Chesnut had other, and in some respects, more serious worries with which to contend. Perhaps these burdens account for the end of Mary's journal: she made no substantive entries after July, 1865 that have survived. Or perhaps the despair and disillusionment created by Southern defeat made such an exercise too painful. Regardless of the reason, one wonders how she reacted to the advent of Radical rule, and other changes in the postwar South. Clues to her opinions can be found in scattered correspondence.

War had left the Chesnuts with virtually no money and many unpaid debts, debts Mary attributed to "the support of our negroes during the war—and before." For the first time in their lives, Mary and James faced real poverty. Such a situation was not uncommon in the South. Most members of the plantation elite had lost substantially as a result of the war. Indeed, Mary's observations about the situation in Camden could have been made anywhere in the immediate post-war South. In Camden, Mary noted, "There are two classes of vociferous sufferers in this community: . . . those who say, 'If people would only pay me what they owe me!' . . . [and] 'If people would only let me alone. I cannot pay them. I could stand it if I had anything to pay debts.' Now we belong to both classes . . . What people owe us and will not or cannot pay would settle all our debts ten times over and leave us in easy circumstances for life. But they will not pay. How can they?" The seemingly constant shortfall in funds and the inability to alleviate that problem would plague the Chesnuts for the rest of their lives.

Unpaid debts and limited financial means were by no means the only consequences of the war. The destruction to the railroads— over two-thirds of the South's 9,000 miles of track had been destroyed—meant a total disruption in commerce, travel, and mail. Those factors produced isolation, a condition which Mary found especially difficult to bear. She wrote in mid-June, 1865: "We are shut in here—turned with our faces to a dead wall. No mails." She would note that "A letter is sometimes brought by a man on horseback," but that letter had to travel "through the wilderness made by Sherman." The situation was, for Mary and others, grim: "We are cut off from the world—to eat out our own hearts."

Given the situation—continued fear of what the Federal authorities would do to her husband and the realization that they had very little money left—it was perhaps natural that Mary would grow even more despondent. She was no different from every other Southerner who had whole-heartedly supported the Confederate war effort and lost everything. Those individuals had often despaired about the Southern cause during the dark days of 1864 and 1865, but the reality of the Confederate defeat was harder than even the most pessimistic had anticipated. Mary's depression deepened as her uncertainty about the future continued. Even a visit to Kamchatka, her old house in Camden, failed to lift her spirits. She noted that:

> I felt so touched & subdued in my old parlours—where I had danced & sung & *acted* & been happy. . . . and there was Mr. Trapier [the current owner] preaching & praying where [children] . . . had played "Puss-in-Boots." I felt sad & tremulous enough— but when Mr. T prayed we might be enabled to bear our bitter disappointment—ruined homes, desolated country, loss of freedom—& then the prayer for him who *was* our ruler [Jefferson Davis], that he might have strength to bear all the tyranny base men could put on him . . .

it was, Mary admitted, too much to bear. She broke down in tears. Later she noted, "I do not think I ever did as much weeping—or as bitter," as during that sad visit to Kamchatka.

Mary's depression continued through the summer. Only gradually, as it became apparent that James would not be arrested, did her despair lift. Still, when Mary wrote to her old friend Virginia Clay in the spring of 1866, traces of her depression were still evident. Mary told Virginia, "We live miles from any body. . . . We are lonely and healthy he[r]e—where neither life nor death seems to matter a great deal." Mary noted that she and James continued to read voraciously, but that literature did not always provide the escape for which she hoped: "[T]here are nights here with the moonlight cold & ghastly & the whippoorwills, & screech owls alone disturbing the silence when I could tear my hair & cry aloud for all that is past & gone." Apparently, Mary attempted to end on a more positive note, for she concluded this candid missive with the statement that "We must not grow weak by vain pining for the past."

The arrival of her favorite nieces and nephews and the need to make a living necessarily forced Mary and James to entertain thoughts other than regret and anger. Money continued to be the most pressing concern—especially after the death of old Colonel Chesnut in February, 1866. James finally inherited the vast Chesnut lands, but it was too late. His father's estate, which included other plantations besides Mulberry, was hopelessly encumbered by debts. By the time the will was probated, James and Mary found themselves in even worse circumstances than before. The reality of the situation forced Mary into channels she would have rejected just a couple of years previously: she set about trying to find some type of work to help her family.

Mary turned first to her former hobby: the butter and egg business she had conducted with her personal servant Molly during the war. Though Molly was a freedwoman now, she returned to Mulberry to work. "As soon as her foot touched her native heath," Mary recalled, "she sent to [sic] hunt up the cattle. Our cows were found in the swamp. . . ." Actually, Mary's working relationship with Molly changed very little: she and Molly had run their little business on shares during the war and they continued to do so now that Molly was free.

As poverty continued to loom large for all the inhabitants of Mulberry, this small cottage industry assumed huge importance, despite James's less than enthusiastic support of it. Mary noted that "My husband and Captain John [Chesnut, her nephew] laugh at my peddling but I notice all of my silver that General Chesnut fails to borrow on Saturday is begged or borrowed by Captain Chesnut by Monday." The products of those animals allowed her and her family a regular, albeit limited, income and a reliable source of food, especially before the railroads to Camden were repaired.

Though the Chesnuts suffered financially throughout this time, they were better off than many in post-war South Carolina. Mulberry, with its fertile lands, and rich variety of crops (a legacy of its antebellum days of self-sufficiency) provided a regular source of food. Mary was gratified to note in late spring that "we have all vegetables in abundance—green peas, asparagus, spring turnips, strawberries, &c, &c. We have so much more than this establishment consumes," she wrote, that she was "enabled to carry baskets of vegetables to my destitute friends." "That," she concluded, "was the one pleasure left me."

Overseeing the butter and egg business, and tending to the plantation's gardens was important, but Mary hoped to find a way to make money doing what she loved most: writing. The choice seemed a natural one. Mary had kept a journal throughout the war, and she had been an avid reader of all types of literature. Further, Mary had several friends and acquaintances who were also embarking upon or continuing literary careers, so it did not seem at all unusual for Mary to pursue a similar endeavor.

Instead of plunging right into writing fiction, Mary began her new vocation by translating works of French literature into English. Given her fluency in the language, it was a natural choice. Her fond hopes of developing a serious career as a writer, however, were put on hold in early 1867. At that time, James, though still barred from office-holding, became even more involved as a behind-the-scenes player in South Carolina Reconstruction politics. As James grew more active politically, he spent less time managing affairs at Mulberry. Because of that, Mary was forced to assume almost all the management and household duties of the plantation. As her responsibilities increased, her time for writing and translating became quite limited.

Mary could not have been blind to the irony of her situation. She had been an observer of plantation affairs for all of her married life. Now, after twenty-seven years, she was in a position to be a true plantation mistress—the role she had been born and bred to assume upon reaching adulthood. But in most ways, it was too late. A plantation mistress' duties, and the daily routine at the estate, had been altered radically, and in many ways, irreparably, by the war. Mary no longer had the wherewithal to organize her home and entertain. Legally, she no longer had a host of enslaved field hands and house servants upon whom to rely. It was a situation that required an incredible amount of attention—and flexibility.

CONDITIONS ON PLANTATIONS THROUGHOUT the South after the war were in flux, and not just because of the Confederate defeat. Emancipation had changed irrevocably the antebellum system of race relations and labor.

News of freedom reached the former slaves at different times and places, and as might be expected, they reacted to that news in a number of ways. One South Carolina slave remembered that " 'some were sorry, some hurt, but a few were silent and glad.' " A former slave on a plantation in Alabama stated that after informed of their freedom, " 'We jes sort of huddle 'round together like scared rabbits, but after we knowed what [the master] mean [sic], didn' many of us go, 'cause we didn' know where to of went.' " Initially, most bondsmen responded to their new status by leaving the plantation to seek relatives from whom they had been separated. Others stayed on at their former masters' plantations, but they refused to work, thus demonstrating tangibly their independence from the master's directives. Those slaves often spoke in anger about past white criticisms of their laziness. They also proved reluctant to farm cotton, the crop they could not divorce from their life of enslavement.

The withdrawal of the region's chief source of labor (a withdrawal economists have calculated equalled anywhere from a 28 percent to 37 percent decline in man hours per capita) convinced Southern state legislatures that they had to institute some rather drastic measures in order to ensure that the spring and fall crops were harvested. Thus, the Black Codes of 1865–1866 were born. These codes varied by state but all were designed to control the freedmen. South Carolina, for example, passed some of the harshest codes that stipulated freedmen had to work in agriculture in some capacity. In general, the codes served to tie the former slaves to the land and thus instituted a system of labor little different from that of slavery.

The freedmen who elected to stay on their masters' farms and plantations did so for a very logical reason. Even without the existence of Black Codes, they had few other options. Years of slavery had trained them for little other than agricultural labor. Most hoped for land and tools to get started in their new lives—as many Northern Radicals had promised. But those dreams died quickly when it became apparent that few politicians would accept or promote the policy of redistributing land confiscated from Southerners during the war. Some freedmen would react to the failure to attain land by moving with their families to the South's urban areas to find employment there. Others sought to take advantage of the 1866 Southern Homestead Act, which did provide land to the freedmen in the public domain of the Southwest. But those who made the journey to Alabama and Mississippi were bitterly disappointed to find that the land offered them was of such poor quality that it was unfit to farm. Many of the freedmen who left in 1865 and 1866 soon returned to their masters' old plantations and sought work for wages.

THE SITUATION AT MULBERRY MIRRORED EVENTS elsewhere in the post-slavery South. Despite the reality of emancipation in the guise of the Thirteenth Amendment, those who had been the Chesnuts' slaves stayed on at Mulberry after the war. From Mary's perspective in May, 1865, the attitude of the freedmen had changed little from before the war. "Everyone has known he or she was free for months, and I do not see one particle of alteration. They are more circumspect, polite and quieter, that's all," she would observe. But, "All goes on—in status quo antebellum. Every day I expect to miss some familiar face. So far, I have been disappointed." On another occasion, she wrote to her friend Virginia Clay that it seemed at times as if they had more black servants than ever before. "Some times [we] do not see a white face for weeks," Mary would note. As if to justify the slaves' pre-war treatment, she went on to add that "the coloured ones hang on like grim death. We will have to run a way [sic] from their persistent devotion—We are free to desert them now I hope." Mary was aware that many in the area around Mulberry loathed losing their slaves. She, however, viewed emancipation differently: "The negroes would be a good riddance." She added bitterly, "A hired man is far cheaper than a man whose father and mother, his wife and his twelve children have to be fed, clothed, housed, nursed, taxes paid and doctor's bills—all for his half-done, slovenly, lazy work." Mary concluded that many Southerners had accepted years ago that "negroes [were] a nuisance that did not pay."

Mary continued to be a keen observer of black actions and attitudes, especially as she became more involved in plantation affairs. She noted that her former slaves were more affectionate and attentive after emancipation than before. She also recorded that the Chesnut freedmen "begged" James to continue to support them which meant, as she had noted previously, yet another financial burden on the already strained Chesnut resources. James did continue to employ his former slaves, but as farm wage laborers instead of slaves. In thus adapting to the law, James and Mary demonstrated how most planter families had to contract with their former slaves in order to obtain their much-needed labor. Mary, however, remarked with a touch of resentment that the freedmen could not hide their disappointment "at not receiving from their friends the Yankees land & money to begin on."

The failure to provide the freedmen with land and tools, and the Radicals' abolishment of the Black Codes forced Southern whites to work out a plan whereby they could get needed labor. The compromise that emerged by 1866 and 1867 was the system of sharecropping. Initially, it seemed like a good solution for both whites and blacks, for it allowed former slaves to work the land in return for a share of the crop they grew, and it provided the planters with the labor they needed. But in the long term, the system would curse the South. It would encourage an increased reliance on staple crop agriculture, which in turn, depleted the soil and led to severe indebtedness when the world's demand for American cotton (which briefly rebounded in 1865), evaporated in the late 1860s. The inflexibility of the system left the South vulnerable when a nation-wide depression struck in 1873, causing increased poverty and a decline in the number of people who owned their land. Neither race escaped the rising tide of poverty and landlessness in the post-war South.

RUNNING A PLANTATION, COPING WITH DISRUPTED race relations, and negotiating contracts with the freedmen—none of these activities was easy in post-Civil War South Carolina and the situation at Mulberry made it an even more demanding task. As time passed, various Chesnut and Miller relations arrived to partake of the hospitality—and relative prosperity—of the Chesnuts. Although the Chesnuts were still hampered by liens against the estate as a result of Colonel Chesnut's death, the land continued to provide ample sources of food. When combined with the butter, eggs, and milk her cows and chickens produced, Mary was able to support her immediate family, as well as all who came for extended visits, and friends in the vicinty.

James's return to politics during the Radical Reconstruction era in 1867 forced Mary to become more involved in the daily management of the Chesnut family holdings. In that year, James served as president of a convention of South Carolinians who gathered in Columbia to protest the advent of military rule. Shortly thereafter, James was sent to the 1868 Democratic National Convention in New York where he supported presidential candidate Horatio Seymour against the Republican candidate, Ulysses S. Grant. Seymour's defeat brought James back to South Carolina where he continued to work tirelessly on behalf of conservative white Democrats against the Radical Republican regime.

OPPOSITION TO THE RADICAL REGIMES BEGAN almost as soon as they attained power in each Southern state. Native Southern whites detested "foreign" rule, and especially, the social and economic policies those governments instituted upon taking office. At the top of the Radical agenda was a campaign of economic and social development. That program was fully in keeping with the Radicals' national crusade to remake the defeated South in the image of the urban-industrial, free labor North. Unfortunately for the Radicals, the Southern states lacked the capital to encourage rebuilding and reinvestment in Southern enterprises. Undaunted by that reality, the Radicals began to use the state governments to aid the quest.

The Republican regimes throughout the South used state bonds to underwrite railroad construction, and liberalized tax laws to encourage Northern businesses to relocate in the former Confederacy. These Radical governments also established public school systems and passed other pieces of social legislation that were designed to help both blacks and poor whites. All these initiatives required money, which was raised by boosting property taxes enormously. This hit the middle-class Southern farmer especially hard at a time when land values were still about half of what they had been before the war. In South Carolina, popular outcries against the wasteful spending of the Radical regime found expression in the Taxpayer's Convention. That movement chose James Chesnut as its leader in 1871.

James served as president of the Taxpayer's Convention in 1871 and again in 1874. In both instances, he spoke out against the extravagant spending and the resort to exorbitant taxation. He corresponded widely with other political leaders outside South Carolina in an attempt to alert them to similar developments in their states. The Taxpayer's Convention eventually entered politics and threw its support to candidates running on independent and reform platforms in the gubernatorial contests of 1874 and 1876. Although the movment was unsuccessful in 1874, it did highlight the growing opposition to the Radical regime in South Carolina.

The Taxpayer's Convention was only one manifestation of discontent with radical rule in South Carolina. Racial violence continued to occur and reached a peak in 1870 and 1871 as the Ku Klux Klan became more active, especially in the South Carolina upcountry. Formed in Pulaski, Tennessee in 1867 as a "fraternal" organization of ex-Confederate soldiers, the Klan quickly became a violent secret order that preyed on the freedmen and all who helped them. Although James was never a member of the Klan, because of his high visibility in state politics he was called upon to testify before a congressional committee that was formed in 1871 to investigate Klan outrages. James used this occasion to disassociate himself from the Klan's violent means and to tell the congressmen what he believed to be the cause of the Klan's renewed activity: the continued presence of "despotic" Radical regimes that were kept in power by military force. White violence against blacks would finally be squelched when President Grant sent more troops to South Carolina in 1871 under the terms of the Force Acts.

James's increased activity in politics meant that he was away from the affairs at Mulberry even more often than before. Although Mary continued to manage the estate quite well, costs continued to burgeon because of increased taxes and the cost of paying wages to the former Chesnut slaves. There was also the problem of the Colonel's will. Under its terms, all the Chesnut lands were to pass intact to a male heir, presumably one of James's nephews. This meant that if James died first, Mary would be dependent upon James's nephews for a place to live. Fear for Mary's future, the cost of maintaining Mulberry and supporting other Chesnut dependents, and James's frequent absences from the plantation all served to convince the Chesnuts that they should build a new home in Camden, with Mary as sole owner. Apparently hoping to save money in the building, the Chesnuts used bricks from the outbuildings at Mulberry to construct the house. That cost-saving measure, however, could not prevent Mary and James from going even deeper into debt. Despite that reality, the house, which Mary helped design and which she named "Sarsfield," was completed in 1873. The Chesnuts left Mulberry shortly thereafter.

Mary delighted in her new house. She had a large first floor bedroom and a library that were all her own and to which she could retreat on the few occasions she had the time to read and write. Mary would rave about her home and would tell her old friend Varina Davis that her favorite room, the library, had a "bay window— filled with Confed[erate] trophys [and] books."

Living in town afforded Mary more socializing opportunities, especially as James continued to be actively involved in state politics. The issue in the mid-1870s continued to be the presence of Radical rule in the state. Conservative opposition to the Republicans had been present since the inception of Radical rule, but not until 1872 did it coalesce under the banner of the Democratic Party.

South Carolina's Democratic Party had crumbled once the Radicals took control. Its reorganization and revival in 1875–1876 marked a significant change in South Carolina politics. Throughout the state's history, representatives from the low-country had dominated most offices, and had played a key role in developing policy stances. The state had, since the nullification crisis, been dominated by Calhounites, though Unionists were a small but vocal minority. Now, however, all Democrats were united in the desire to restore "home rule" to South Carolina. Demonstrating a unity not seen since the days of Calhoun and nullification, Democrats set their sights on the 1876 gubernatorial contest.

The Chesnuts were active observers of and participants in the canvass. Both had known the Democratic candidate, Wade Hampton, for years. The contest, between Hampton and Republican Daniel Chamberlain was a bitterly fought one that was marked by fraud, corruption, and violence. Both sides disputed the final results, and claimed victory, which led to the establishment of dual state governments in Columbia.

The contest between Chamberlain and Hampton was played out against the backdrop of the national presidential election of 1876. That election, waged between Republican Rutherford B. Hayes and Democrat Samuel J. Tilden, was also marked by violence—and by a set of disputed election returns in the three states where Radical Republican regimes remained in power: South Carolina, Louisiana, and Florida (Oregon also posted disputed returns which, if accepted, would have taken away the one vote that eventually allowed Hayes's victory). Congress attempted to end the impasse by appointing a bipartisan electoral commission to investigate the elections in those three Southern states. The commission, however, was composed of eight Republicans and seven Democrats. As they sifted through the returns, time became a factor. Tilden remained aloof from the proceedings, but representatives of the Hayes camp contacted leading Democrats from South Carolina (including Wade Hampton) and Louisiana about what a Republican administration with Hayes at the helm would mean for the South. Other Hayes supporters and the Southerners also discussed economic issues that might affect the region (in particular a Southern transcontinental railroad) during this time.

As it became apparent that the electoral commission would award the disputed votes to Hayes, Tilden's supporters threatened to hold up the inauguration via a series of parliamentary maneuvers. Apparently undaunted by that threat, Hayes's lieutenants arranged for a final series of meetings with some representatives from the South in late February, 1877, at Washington's Wormeley House hotel. At that meeting, Hayes's agents promised that federal intervention in Southern affairs would come to an end. By that time, it was clear that Hayes would be sworn in as president in March.

Scholars still debate the results of this so-called Compromise of 1877. Most of the key negotiations were in secret, so it is very difficult to discern what was discussed and promised. Hayes, however, did emerge victorious in the election, and he did order federal troops guarding the rival Republican state governments in South Carolina and Louisiana to leave. But Hayes did not order the removal of all federal troops. Regardless, the withdrawal had the desired effect: in April, 1877, the Radical Republican regime in South Carolina collapsed. The next day, Wade Hampton was duly inaugurated as the state's lone governor. Southern Democratic "Redemption" had been achieved.

To be sure, James and Mary were delighted to see their old friend and political ally installed in the governor's office. They were also gratified to have the hated Republicans ousted from their state. But their hopes that the return of Democratic rule would aid James's political career came to naught. James had been told that he would be appointed to a post on a federal tariff commission in the early 1880s (he had asked Congress in 1878 to remove his remaining disqualifications for office holding and it had accepted his request), but that promise was never fulfilled. Although he remained active politically, he would never again be a public servant. Instead, he spent his final years reading, writing, and collecting documents for his memoirs.

WITH JAMES'S RETIREMENT FROM POLITICAL LIFE, Mary was able to return to her own writing. It was during this time, in the late 1870s, that she began to experiment with writing fiction. The novels that resulted from her efforts were based loosely on her life and the experiences of her family. Her first attempts, entitled "We Called her Kitty" and "Two Years of My Life," dealt with her childhood and schooling at Madame Talvande's. Mary's other attempt at fiction was "The Captain and the Colonel," a Civil War tale based on the military adventures of her beloved nephew Johnny Chesnut. She also wrote a short story, "The Arrest of a Spy," for the *Charleston News and Courier*. For that piece she was paid $10, which was probably the only money she ever received for her literary efforts. In addition to novels and short stories, Mary penned short biographical sketches of James for inclusion in volumes dealing with prominent South Carolinians. She relished the return to this much loved activity, but she would again be stymied in its pursuit. Just as she began to get involved deeply in her work Mary would be hit hard by a series of family illnesses, deaths, and financial reversals.

Mary's string of tragedies began in mid-1875, when James was gored by a bull and seriously injured. His recovery took months, and Mary nursed him the entire time. While she ministered to James, she received word that her favorite sister Kate had died. Mary had just begun to digest that information when she was notified that Kate's daughter, her favorite niece Serena, had also passed away. This double blow plunged Mary into a deep depression that many within her family feared she would never shake. Accompanying her depression was a deteriorating heart condition, with the result that from 1876 until her death, Mary would always be troubled by angina.

The Chesnut finances continued to be a source of concern, and forced Mary, once she was able to get beyond her grief, to seize control of the family finances. As during the last year of the war, she was forced into a rigid accounting of virtually every penny. She was especially disturbed that their reduced circumstances kept her from indulging in one of her favorite loves: buying books. Mary would work around this by starting a book club with friends and family members. This allowed her to take her mind off her grief by immersing herself in the latest magazines and works of literature.

Mary would return to her writing when she could, but after 1876, she moved away from her attempts at fiction and turned instead to her Civil War journals. Many of those daybooks were still stuffed with bits of paper, letters, and random notes. Mary often found herself too busy at a particular moment to jot down all she had done or seen. The pieces of miscellany she had squirrled away were intended to help refresh her memory once she did have the occasion to compile her observations about the events of a specific day. Now that she had the time, Mary decided to fill in some of the gaps that she had left during the war.

She managed to carry on with this work off and on for almost ten years before tragedy once again intervened. In January of 1885, James suffered a stroke, and shortly thereafter, Mary's mother, who had been living with the Chesnuts, also fell ill. Mary spent weeks ministering to both, and her exertions seriously affected her own rather precarious health. On February 1, 1885, at the age of seventy, James died. Mary had barely accepted that reality when her mother passed away a few days later. The loss of the two people closest to her heart affected her deeply. She was now alone, except for some nieces and nephews. James had made Mary the sole beneficiary of his estate, but by 1885, it amounted to little more than her title to Sarsfield. Widowed and almost penniless, she had little to which to look forward. An entry in her daybook for 1885 testified to her woe: "February 1885—the black year of my life."

Though sixty-two years old herself and sickened with grief, Mary worked energetically to overcome the burdens that she inherited. She became embroiled in legal battles over James's will for months, and was forced to deal with various liens against her property and income—limited though it was. As a result, she became ever more dependent upon her butter and egg business, and was forced unwillingly to contact various relatives to urge them to pay her back the money she and James had loaned them in earlier times. Few could have imagined that Mary Chesnut, once wife of one of the wealthiest men in South Carolina was, by the end of 1885, living on an annual income of $140.

Despite having experienced hard times for over twenty years since the end of the war, Mary kept her humor and her strength. She had survived war and was surviving poverty. Depression continued to affect her from time to time, but she kept going. The strong, independent spirit that had made her so indomitable throughout her life continued to hold her in good stead. Still, her heart, never strong, weakened considerably after James's death. Realizing that she was in declining health, she discussed with her young friend Isabella Martin the publication of her journals if she did not live to do it herself.

Mary would not survive to see her diaries published. In November, 1886, she caught a cold. Her aunt, Charlotte Boykin Taylor, tried to nurse her back to health, but the infection seemed to spread rapidly to her lungs. Ultimately, it was her heart that gave out. On November 22, 1886, Mary Boykin Chesnut finally lost her battle against heart disease and succumbed to death. She was buried on a cold, rainy day, at Knight's Hill in Camden, next to James.

MARY CHESNUT'S DEATH REPRESENTED an end to the Old South—arguably as much a milestone as events at Shiloh, Gettysburg, or Appomatox, or the passage of the Thirteenth Amendment. Born into an aristocratic life of ease, Mary Chesnut was swept into a whirlwind of events over which she had little control. The war changed her life as dramatically as it had altered the nation. That she was able to pick up the pieces as well as she did is testimony to her strength and perseverance.

As a women in a world that did not recognize or encourage strong women, Mary Chesnut stands out as a survivor. That she recorded her own story in a diary is evidence that she understood her own self-worth. In a moment of frustration and perhaps even doubt she questioned, "Why was I born so frightfully ambitious?" A century later we can be thankful she was.

Epilogue

———————◯———————

The Diary from Dixie

ON FEBRUARY 23, 1865, WHILE STILL IN EXILE in Lincolnton, North Carolina, Mary Chesnut wrote: "Today is Thursday & for four days I have not written. I have been busily engaged—reading the *10* volumes of *memoirs* of the times I have written. Nearly all my sage prophecies have been verified the wrong way—& every insight into character or opinion I have given as to men turned out utter folly. Still I write on—for if I have to burn—& here lie my treasures ready for the blazing hearth—still they have served to while away fo[u]r days of agony." Little could she have known just how lucky posterity was that she did not toss those ten books into the fire. Over the course of the four years of the war, Mary had destroyed parts of her journal—when Federal troops threatened, for example. But for the most part, in 1865 Mary's account of life in the inner circle of the Confederacy was intact.

Mary's interest in literature and literary endeavors was lifelong. She always toyed with the idea of writing and enjoyed her numerous forays into the world of writing fiction. But eventually she turned to her own reminiscences of the great and exciting period from 1861 to 1865. Mary was well aware that parts of the diary were blank; she herself had noted on September 23, 1863, that "I destroyed all my

notes and journal—from the time I arrived at Flat Rock—during a
raid upon Richmond in 1863. Afterward—I tried to fill up the gap
from memory." To aid her in the reconstruction of her experiences at
a later time, she had jotted down brief notes, and had collected
items to help jog her memory. All these scraps were thrown together
in her daybooks.

Mary was also keenly aware that parts of her journals were
unusually candid. (She had, at times, kept her journals "under lock
and key," but often was dismayed to find even that security breached
by carelessness). Perhaps because of that candor, she knew that
some careful editing would have to take place before their publication, so as not to offend old friends and acquaintances. The gaps,
the blunt and catty comments, the brief sketches of momentous
developments in Richmond and elsewhere—all these elements
convinced Mary that a substantive revision of her journals was
needed before they could be presented to a wider audience. Little
did she realize that later historians would regard her "candor" as one
of the more charming and informative features of the journal.

Beginning in the mid-1870s, Mary began the task of revising.
Armed with pencil and eraser, she tackled the more critical remarks
about some of the Confederacy's more famous personalities. During
that period she probably revised or re-wrote about 400 pages of the
original manuscript. But other concerns, most notably James's ill
health in 1875, necessarily side-tracked her efforts, and she did not
resume her work on the diaries again until 1881.

Mary did not abandon writing entirely during the period from
1875 and 1881, however. Those were the years during which she
penned her autobiographical accounts, "Two Years of My Life," and
"We called her Kitty," as well as the novel "The Captain and the
Colonel." According to the leading authority on Mary's writings, that
period of her work marked her "apprenticeship" in writing. It was
while she described her early life and while she created a Civil War
novel that she refined the style she would introduce to her journals
in the 1880s. Those journals, which she tackled anew in 1881,
dominated the last five years of her life.

The more Mary fleshed out, the longer the journals became. At
one point, in June of 1883, she wrote to her dear friend Varina Davis
about her project: "How I wish you could read over—my Journal—

I have been two years over looking it [sic]—copying—leaving myself out. You must see it before it goes to print—but that may not be just now. I mean the printing—for I must over haul it again—and again." According to this missive, Mary anticipated a protracted period of writing and revising. By that time, she had already filled dozens of copybooks with her reminiscences.

Mary's fond hopes of uninterrupted work on her journals were dashed by more heartache. James and her mother's illnesses distracted her and by 1885, forced her to put away her writing in order to nurse them. Perhaps Mary realized she would never have the opportunity to finish her revisions, for she discussed with her young friend Isabella Martin the possibility that Isabella would arrange for their eventual publication.

Family tragedies, continued poverty, and her own ill health prevented Mary from completing her journals before her death in 1886. Her nephew, David R. Williams III, inherited what little was left of Mary's estate, including her journals. He kept them, and eventually turned them over to Isabella Martin, who put them away for many years. Finally, in 1904, writer and editor Myrta Lockett Avary contacted Isabella about Mary Chesnut's journals. Working together, Isabella and Myrta Avary undertook yet another rewrite of the Chesnut diaries. The version they edited appeared in 1905 and was entitled *A Diary From Dixie*.

But that was not the last of Mary Chesnut's journals. Novelist Ben Ames Williams became captivated with the 1905 edition while he was doing research for his own Civil War novel, *A House Divided*. In 1949, he, too, published a revision of the Chesnut diaries, also entitled *A Diary From Dixie*. Williams's version edited out even more than Isabella Martin and Myrta Avary had. The novelist also undertook some rather substantive re-writing. Once published, the Williams version of the Chesnut diaries stood as a major primary source on the Confederacy for almost forty years.

Mary Chesnut's original journals and daybooks ultimately found a home at the University of South Carolina's South Caroliniana Library. During a term in residence, noted Southern historian C. Vann Woodward collected all of Mary's writings and undertook the herculean task of reading and editing the original volumes Mary Chesnut had written and revised. Published in 1982, *Mary Chesnut's*

Civil War presented Mary's journals as she herself left them after all her tinkerings in the 1880s. Two years later, with the aid of Elisabeth Muhlenfeld, Woodward also edited Mary's original, extant, and unedited diaries dating from 1861 and 1865, and published them under the title *The Private Mary Chesnut: The Unpublished Civil War Diaries*. Finally, almost one hundred years after her death, scholars and buffs were rewarded with two editions that contained all that Mary Chesnut had originally written, edited, and re-written between the years 1861 and 1885.

Historians have questioned just how reliable Mary Chesnut's diary is. It was, after all, revised, and in some areas written years after the events it reports took place. Still, Woodward and others have argued that Mary's revisions were scrupulously honest to the historical record; Woodward himself notes in his preface to *Mary Chesnut's Civil War* that during the course of his editing he was impressed with the "integrity" of Mary's writing. She may have toned down some of her more caustic comments, but her report of various events remains true to history. Her efforts to be "entirely *objective*" in many ways succeeded.

Mary Chesnut's account of the Confederacy from its birth to its tortured death provides us an intimate look into the lives of elite white Southerners. She speaks on a variety of topics, and throughout, educates and entertains us. Her views are not really representative of the general population; nor can she be viewed as a typical nineteenth century Southern women. Still, her opinions and perceptions give us a far keener sense of what it was like for wealthy white Southerners to watch their way of life be challenged and destroyed. Few others could tell us this story as poignantly and as well.

Perhaps it is fitting that we still look to Mary Chesnut's views of the old South and the Civil War for insight into those four cataclysmic years. Given her penchant for history and literature, not to mention good conversation and debate, she undoubtedly would be pleased to see the continued popularity of her diary. Mary Chesnut has attained, through the posthumous publication of her journals, the type of fame and notoriety she would have relished in her lifetime.

Suggested Reading

THE BEST PLACE TO BEGIN A STUDY OF MARY CHESNUT is with her diaries. C. Vann Woodward's *Mary Chesnut's Civil War* (New Haven, 1981) is a Pulitzer Prize winning edition of all of Mary's wartime journals. The unpublished, original journals, dating from 1861 and 1865, have also been edited by Woodward and Elisabeth Muhlenfeld, and are entitled, *The Private Mary Chesnut: The Unpublished Civil War Diaries* (New York, 1984). The original Chesnut manuscripts, as well as several collections of Chesnut family papers, may be found at the South Caroliniana Library at the University of South Carolina in Columbia. Other works dealing with the Chesnut family and antebellum and wartime South Carolina may be viewed at the South Carolina Historical Society in Charleston.

The field of Southern women's history is a burgeoning one. Those interested in the life of a Southern lady are encouraged to consult Catherine Clinton's *The Plantation Mistress: Woman's World in the Old South* (New York: 1982), as well as an anthology of essays she edited, entitled, *Half Sisters of History: Southern Women and the American Past* (Durham, 1994). Also of note is Elizabeth Fox-Genovese's *Within the Plantation Household: Black and White Women of the Old South* (Chapel Hill, 1988), which juxtaposes the plantation experiences of white women and their slaves. Jane Turner Censer has explored the family life of planters in order to discern how and where cultural values were transmitted in *North Carolina Planters and Their Children, 1800–1860* (Baton Rouge, 1984). Jean E.

Friedman's *The Enclosed Garden: Women and Community in the Evangelical South, 1830–1900* studies how the social structure, Victorian culture, the evangelical tradition, and close female ties affected women throughout the prewar and postwar periods. The idea of Southern families, gender relations, and socialization is covered in Steven Stowe's *Intimacy and Power in the Old South: Ritual in the Lives of the Planters* (Baltimore, 1987). Finally, no study of Southern women and families would be complete without Bertram Wyatt-Brown's *Southern Honor: Ethics and Behavior in the Old South* (New York, 1982). Although Wyatt-Brown's emphasis is on Southern men and the ethic of honor, he includes several chapters detailing the patriarchal side of Southern honor and how it affected male-female relationships in the antebellum South.

South Carolina's unique history has been studied extensively. A good place to start understanding the Palmetto State's radicalism is in William W. Freehling's *Prelude to Civil War: The Nullification Controversy in South Carolina, 1816–1836* (New York, 1966), and Lacy K. Ford's *Origins of Southern Radicalism: The South Carolina Upcountry, 1800–1860* (New York, 1988). South Carolina politics during the late antebellum period have been analyzed by John Barnwell, *Love of Order: South Carolina's First Secession Crisis* (Chapel Hill, 1982) and *Nationalism and Sectionalism in South Carolina, 1852–1860: A Study in the Movement for Independence* (Durham, 1950), by Harold S. Schultz. Steven Channing's *Crisis of Fear: Secession in South Carolina* (New York, 1974), traces the state's final push into secession. Readers interested in a more general account of the South's course to secession should consult William W. Freehling's *Road to Disunion: Secessionists At Bay, 1776–1854* (New York, 1990), or the older but still valuable *The Impending Crisis, 1848–1861* (New York, 1976) by David M. Potter.

There is no dearth of books on the Confederate experience. The best general overview of the war years is found in Emory M. Thomas's *The Confederate Nation, 1861–1865* (New York, 1979). Charles Edward Cauthen's *South Carolina Goes to War, 1860–1865* (Chapel Hill, 1950) presents a narrative of the state's wartime experiences. For an excellent biography of President Jefferson Davis, which includes numerous references to Mary Chesnut, see William

C. Davis, *Jefferson Davis, The Man and His Hour: A Biography* (New York, 1991). Davis's new book, *"A Government of Our Own": The Making of the Confederacy* (New York, 1994) is a wonderful account of the Confederacy's early days in Montgomery. Also of note is George C. Rable's *The Confederate Republic: A Revolution Against Politics* (Chapel Hill, 1994), which presents a thoughtful and different interpretation of Confederate politics and their effect on the Confederacy.

The role of women in the Confederacy's drive for independence has become a popular topic among Southern historians. George C. Rable's *Civil Wars: Women and the Crisis of Southern Nationalism* (Urbana and Chicago, 1989) is an impressive analysis of how women reacted to the war in all its phases. A volume of essays on related topics has been compiled by Catherine Clinton and Nina Silber and is entitled, *Divided Houses: Gender and the Civil War* (New York, 1992). Anne Firor Scott's now classic *The Southern Lady: From Pedestal to Politics* (Durham, 1972) talks about how revolutionary the war was for Southern women, an interpretation that has been modified by Clinton, Rable, and others.

Much of the best recent scholarship on the Confederacy focuses upon the internal breakdown of the nation. Paul D. Escott's *After Secession: Jefferson Davis and the Failure of Confederate Nationalism* (Baton Rouge, 1978) explores class conflict and Confederate defeat. Rable's book, too, focuses on the class dimensions of Confederate defeat.

Civil War diaries and memoirs are a staple of the historiography. Unfortunately, sources on the lives of the yeomanry are sparse; hence, there is a definite class bias to the diaries and journals that are extant. Nonetheless, one interested in comparing Mary Chesnut's experiences with other Southern women, wealthy and otherwise, would be wise to consult Phoebe Yates Pember's *A Southern Woman's Story* (Jackson, Tenn., 1959) as well as Virginia Clay-Clopton's *A Belle of the Fifties: Memoirs of Mrs. Clay of Alabama Covering Social and Political Life in Washington and the South, 1853-1866* (New York, 1904, 1969), Constance Cary Harrison's *Recollections Grave and Gay* (New York, 1911), and Judith McGuire's, *Diary of a Southern Refugee* (New York, 1867, 1972). Michael Manson Myers has edited a substantial volume of the correspondence carried out among members of the wealthy Jones family in neighboring Georgia. Entitled *The Children of Pride* (New Haven, 1972), Myers presents a good counterpart family to the Chesnut clan in another Southern state. Other wartime accounts that contrast with Chesnut's carefree and comfortable life may be found in J. B. Jones's *A Rebel War Clerk's Diary* (Philadelphia, 1866, New York, 1935) and Edward Younger, ed., *Inside the Confederate Government: The Diary of Robert Hill Garlick Kean* (New York, 1957).

The military side of the Civil War has attracted legions of chroniclers. Those interested in a comprehensive overview should consult Shelby Foote's three-volume narrative, *The Civil War* (New York, 1958–1974). Thomas L. Connelly's two volume study of the Confederate Army of Tennessee, *Army of the Heartland: The Army of Tennessee, 1861–1862* (Baton Rouge, 1967) and *Autumn of Glory: The Army of Tennessee, 1862–1865* (Baton Rouge, 1971) provides a detailed view of the Confederacy's war in the west. Students interested in Sherman and his 1864–1865 campaigns in Georgia and South Carolina should also see John F. Marszalek's *Sherman: A Soldier's Passion For Order* (New York, 1993) and Charles Royster's *The Destructive War: William Tecumseh Sherman, Stonewall Jackson, and the Americans* (New York, 1991).

The saga of Reconstruction has also been the subject of numerous historical studies. The best synthesis and interpretation is found in Eric Foner's *Reconstruction: America's Unfinished Revolution, 1863–1877* (New York, 1988). Sadly, no one has tackled South Carolina's history of Reconstruction since Francis Butler Simkins and Robert Hilliard Woody's *South Carolina During Reconstruction* (Chapel Hill, 1932). However, William J. Cooper has explored the state's period of Redemption and the advent of Conservative rule in *The Conservative Regime: South Carolina, 1877-1890* (Baltimore, 1968). Joel Williamson's *After Slavery: The Negro in South Carolina During Reconstruction, 1861–1877* (Chapel Hill, 1965) is a solid account of the freedmen in the state. For a detailed analysis of the workings of the Freedmen's Bureau, see Martin Abbott, *The Freedmen's Bureau in South Carolina, 1865–1872* (Chapel Hill, 1967).

The economic impact of emancipation upon the freedmen and white Southerners has also garnered a good deal of attention. Roger Ransom and Richard Sutch have written an excellent study of the effect of war and emancipation on the Southern economy in *One Kind of Freedom: The Economic Consequences of Emancipation* (New York, 1977). See as well Gavin Wright's *Political Economy of the Cotton South: Households, Markets, and Wealth In the Nineteenth Century* (New York, 1978). For the freedmen's reaction to the end of their bondage, see Leon Litwack's *Been in the Storm so Long: The Aftermath of Slavery* (New York, 1979).

Mary Chesnut has been the subject of a number of articles, masters' theses, and dissertations. Some of her letters, which are scattered in various repositories around the South, have been collected and transcribed by Allie Patricia Wall in her master's thesis, "The Letters of Mary Boykin Chesnut," (University of South Carolina, 1977). Elisabeth Muhlenfeld's doctoral dissertation, "Mary Boykin Chesnut: The Writer and Her Work" (University of South Carolina, 1978) contains typescripts of the novels Chesnut penned after the war. Muhlenfeld's revised dissertation, published as *Mary Boykin Chesnut: A Biography* (Baton Rouge, 1981) is the only other full length account of this fascinating woman. Muhlenfeld's emphasis is on Chesnut's writing and the evolution from her literary endeavors to her diary.

Index